On Mental Illness

The School of Life

Published in 2022 by The School of Life
First published in the USA in 2022
930 High Road, London, N12 9RT

Designed by Marcia Mihotich
Typeset by Kerrypress
Printed in Latvia by Livonia

A proportion of this book has appeared online at www.theschooloflife.com/thebookoflife

The School of Life is a resource for helping us understand ourselves, for improving our relationships, our careers and our social lives – as well as for helping us find calm and get more out of our leisure hours. We do this through creating films, workshops, books, apps and gifts.

www.theschooloflife.com

ISBN 978-1-912891-81-8

10 9 8 7 6 5 4 3 2 1

Contents

Introduction

For a long time, we may cope well enough. We make it to work every morning, we give pleasant summaries of our lives to friends, we smile over dinner. We aren't totally balanced, but there's no good way of knowing how difficult things might be for other people, and what we might have a right to expect in terms of contentment and peace of mind. We probably tell ourselves to stop being self-indulgent and redouble our efforts to feel worthy through achievement. We are probably world experts in not feeling sorry for ourselves.

Decades may pass. It's not uncommon for the most serious mental conditions to remain undiagnosed for half a lifetime. We simply don't notice that we are, beneath the surface, chronically anxious, filled with self-loathing and close to overwhelming despair and rage. This too simply ends up feeling normal.

Then, one day, something triggers a collapse. It might be a crisis at work, a reversal in our career plans or a mistake we've made over a task. It might be a romantic failure, someone leaving us or a realisation that we are profoundly unhappy with a partner we had thought might be our long-term future. Alternatively, we feel mysteriously exhausted and sad, to the extent that we can't face anything any more, even a family meal or a conversation with a friend. Or we are struck by unmanageable anxiety around everyday challenges, like addressing our colleagues or going into a shop. We're swamped by a sense of doom and imminent catastrophe. We sob uncontrollably.

We are in a mental crisis. If we are lucky, we will put up the white flag at once. There is nothing shameful or rare in our condition; we have fallen ill, as so many before us have. We need not compound our sickness with a sense of embarrassment. This is what happens when one is a delicate human facing the hurtful, alarming and always uncertain conditions of existence. Recovery can start the moment one admits one no longer has a clue how to cope.

The roots of the crisis almost certainly go a long way back. Things will not have been right in certain areas for an age, possibly forever. There will have been grave inadequacies in the early days, things that were said and done to us that should never have occurred and bits of reassurance and care that were ominously missed out on. On top of this, adult life will have layered on difficulties that we were not well equipped to know how to endure. It will have applied pressure along our most tender, invisible fault lines.

Our illness is trying to draw attention to our problems, but it can only do so inarticulately, by throwing up coarse and vague symptoms. It knows how to signal that we are worried and sad, but it can't tell us what about and why. That will be the work of patient investigation, over months and years, probably in the company of experts. The illness contains the cure, but it has to be teased out and its original inarticulacy interpreted. Something from the past is crying out to be recognised and will not leave us alone until we have given it its due.

At points, it may seem like a death sentence, but beneath the crisis we are being given an opportunity to restart our lives on a more generous, kind and realistic footing. We should dare to listen to what our pain is trying to tell us.

***

Mental health is a miracle we are apt not to notice until it slips from our grasp – at which point we may wonder how we ever managed to do anything as complicated and beautiful as order our thoughts sanely and calmly.

A mind in a healthy state is, in the background, continually performing a near-miraculous set of manoeuvres that underpin our moods of clear-sightedness and purpose. To appreciate what mental health involves (and therefore what makes up its opposite), we should take a moment to consider some of what will be happening in the folds of an optimally functioning mind.

First and foremost, a healthy mind is an *editing* mind, an organ that manages to sieve, from thousands of stray, dramatic, disconcerting or horrifying thoughts, those particular ideas and sensations that actively need to be entertained in order for us to direct our lives effectively.

Partly this means keeping at bay punitive and critical judgements that might want to tell us repeatedly how disgraceful and appalling we are, long after harshness has ceased to serve any useful purpose. When we are interviewing for a new job or taking someone on a date, a healthy mind doesn't force us to listen to inner voices that insist on our unworthiness. It allows us to talk to ourselves as we would to a friend.

At the same time, a healthy mind resists the pull of unfair comparisons. It doesn't constantly allow the achievements and successes of others to throw us off course and reduce us to a state of bitter inadequacy. It doesn't torture us by continually comparing our condition to that of people who have, in reality, had very different upbringings and trajectories through life. A well-functioning mind recognises the futility and cruelty of constantly finding fault with its own nature.

Along the way, a healthy mind keeps a judicious grip on the faucet of fear. It knows that, in theory, there is an endless number of things that we could worry about: a blood vessel might fail, a scandal might erupt, the plane's engines could shear from their wings … But it has a good sense of the distinction between what could *conceivably* happen and what is in fact *likely* to happen. It is able to leave us in peace as regards the wilder eventualities of fate, confident that awful things will either not unfold or could be dealt with ably enough if ever they did so. A healthy mind avoids catastrophic imaginings: it knows that there are broad and stable stone steps, not a steep and slippery incline, between itself and disaster.

A healthy mind has compartments with heavy doors that shut securely. It can compartmentalise where it needs to. Not all thoughts belong at all moments. While talking to a grandmother, the mind prevents the emergence of images of last night's erotic fantasies; while looking after a child, it can repress its more cynical and misanthropic analyses. Aberrant thoughts about jumping on a train line or harming oneself with a sharp knife can remain brief, peculiar flashes rather than repetitive fixations. A healthy mind has mastered the techniques of censorship.

A healthy mind can quieten its own buzzing preoccupations in order, at times, to focus on the world beyond itself. It can be present and engaged with what and who is immediately around. Not everything it could feel has to be felt at every moment.

A healthy mind combines an appropriate suspicion of certain people with a fundamental trust in humanity. It can take an intelligent risk with a stranger. It doesn't extrapolate from life's worst moments in order to destroy the possibility of connection.

A healthy mind knows how to hope; it identifies and then tenaciously hangs on to a few reasons to keep going. Grounds for despair, anger and sadness are, of course, all around. But the healthy mind knows how to bracket negativity in the name of endurance. It clings to evidence of what is still good and kind. It remembers to appreciate; it can – despite everything – still look forward to a hot bath, some dried fruit or dark chocolate, a chat with a friend or a satisfying day of work. It refuses to let itself be silenced by all the many sensible arguments in favour of rage and despondency.

Outlining some of the features of a healthy mind helps us to identify what can go awry when we fall ill; at the heart of mental illness is a loss of control over our own better thoughts and feelings. An unwell mind can't apply a filter to the information that reaches our awareness; it can no longer order or sequence its content. From this, any number of painful scenarios ensue.

Ideas keep coming to the fore that serve no purpose, and unkind voices echo ceaselessly. Worrying possibilities press on us all at once, without any bearing on the probability of their occurrence. Fear runs riot.

Simultaneously, regrets drown out any capacity to make our peace with who we are. Every bad thing we have ever said or done reverberates and cripples our self-esteem. We are unable to assign correct proportions to anything: a drawer that doesn't open feels like a conclusive sign that we are doomed; a slightly unfriendly remark by an acquaintance becomes proof that we shouldn't exist. We can't grade our worries and zero in on the few that might truly deserve concern.

We can't temper our sadness. We cannot overcome the idea that we have not been loved properly, that we have made a mess of the whole of our working lives, that we have disappointed everyone who ever had faith in us.

Every compartment of the mind is blown open. The strangest, most extreme thoughts run unchecked across consciousness. We begin to fear that we might shout obscenities in public or do harm with the kitchen knives.

In the worst cases, we lose the power to distinguish outer reality from our inner world. We can't tell what is outside of us and what is inside, where we end and others begin; we speak to people as if they were actors in our own dreams.

At night, such is the maelstrom and the ensuing exhaustion, we become defenceless before our worst apprehensions. By 3 a.m., after hours of rumination, doing away with ourselves no longer feels like a remote or unwelcome notion.

However dreadful this sounds, a paradox is that, for the most part, mental illness from the outside tends not to look as dramatic as we think it might. The majority of us, when we are mentally unwell, will not be foaming at the mouth or insisting that we are Napoleon. We won't be making speeches about alien invasions or declaring that we control space and time. Our suffering will be quieter, more inward, more concealed and more contiguous with societal norms; we'll sob mutely into the pillow or dig our nails silently into our palms. Others may not even realise for a long time, if ever, that we are in difficulty. We ourselves may not accept the scale of our sickness.

The dated and clichéd images of 'madness' – with their obscenities, ravings and bombast – may be frightening in themselves, but our collective focus on them suggests a concealed search for reassurance. We depict mental illness in colourful and extreme terms to convince ourselves of our own sanity; to put some clear blue water between our own fragile states and those of people dismissively termed 'lunatics'. We thereby fail to acknowledge the extent to which mental illness is ultimately as common, and as essentially unshameful, as its bodily counterpart – and also comprises a host of more minor ailments, the equivalents of cold sores and broken wrists, abdominal cramps or ingrowing toenails.

When we define mental illness as a loss of command over the mind, few of us can claim to be free of all instances of unwellness. True mental health involves a frank acceptance of how much ill health there will have to be in even the most ostensibly competent and meaningful lives. There will be days when we simply can't stop crying over someone we have lost. Or when we worry so much about the future, we wish that we hadn't been born. Or when we feel so sad, it seems futile even to open our mouths. At such times, we should be counted as no less ill than a person laid up in bed with flu – and as worthy of attention and sympathy.

It doesn't help our fears that we are at least a hundred years away from properly fathoming how the brain operates – and how it might be healed. We are in the mental arena roughly equivalent to where we might have been in bodily medicine around the middle of the 17th century, as we slowly built up a picture of how blood circulated around our veins or how our kidneys functioned. In our attempts to find fixes, we are akin to those surgeons depicted in early prints who cut up cadavers with rusty scissors and clumsily dug around innards with a poker. We might be well on the way to colonising Mars before we definitively grasp the secrets to the workings of our own minds.

We are not especially stupid, but what we are dealing with is uncommonly abstruse. We get a sense of this at moments when the mind hints at its underlying depths; for example, as we fall asleep and behold voices and images from different periods of our lives – and feel just how densely packed and continually and manically observant our minds are, how much they have stored and how many pains and inchoate longings remain locked inside us.

Looking at the paintings of the American artist Cy Twombly (1928–2011), we might derive a particular feeling for the intricacies of certain mental processes that are normally tidied away before we speak; it is as if Twombly were showing us what ordinary consciousness might look like in its raw state. His art moves us by the honesty of its intimate portraiture of inner reality. We might wonder, given the tumult within, how we ever manage to sound even slightly coherent or focused, and acquire a new awe at the miraculous, flawed, brilliant organs through which we are compelled to steer our always unsteady path through existence.

For most of history, the only help on offer for our ailing minds was grotesque in nature. Just as primitive medicine made us endure leeches and anaesthetic-free amputations, so early psychiatry suggested electric shocks and random incisions in our frontal lobes. More commonly, we were tied to a wall in a prison-like clinic and left to scream. Only gradually did we learn to approach our mental troubles with humanity and care, and recognise that the apparently insane were merely ailing versions of us all, only particularly deserving of love and gentleness.

This book sets out to consider, with modesty and compassion, how we might best approach some of our states of mental

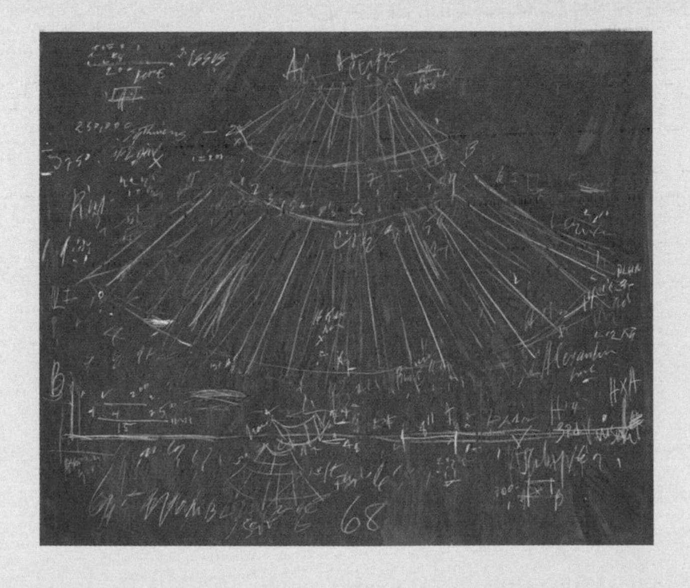

Cy Twombly, *Synopsis of a Battle*, 1968

Tony Robert-Fleury, *Dr. Philippe Pinel at the Salpêtrière*, 1795. This painting depicts Pinel ordering the removal of chains from patients at the Paris Asylum for Insane Women.

unwellness. It outlines a number of strategies – fourteen in all – that we might adopt in a search for calm, respite and consolation.

It is surely no coincidence that in many parts of Europe, asylums for the mentally ill were, from the Renaissance onwards, opened up in converted monasteries, signalling an implicit connection between the solace sought from religion and from psychiatry. The best of these asylums (and there were very few) promised a dignified refuge from the pressures of society and the terrors of the mind. They may have had extensive gardens – most famously like the one at the Saint-Paul Asylum in Saint-Rémy, where an ailing Vincent van Gogh spent a year in 1889, sitting very still in his room for hours at a time and then painting dozens of sublime canvases of irises, cypresses and pine trees – that may to this day help to persuade the inconsolable to keep living.

Vincent van Gogh, *The Garden of Saint-Paul Hospital*, 1889

In its way, this book aims to be a sanctuary, a walled garden filled with nourishing psychological vegetation, and with comfortable benches on which to sit and recover our strength, in an atmosphere of kindness and fellow-feeling. It outlines a raft of therapeutic moves with which we might approach our most stubborn mental afflictions and instabilities. It sets out to be a friend through some of the most difficult moments of our lives.

Therapeutic Moves

1.
Reasons to Live

When we are feeling well in our minds, we hardly notice that we might be harbouring in ourselves anything as formal or as dramatic-sounding as 'reasons to live'. We simply assume that we like life itself and that it must be natural and inevitable to do so. Yet a broad appetite for life is, on close inspection, never simply that; our apparently general buoyancy covertly rests on a range of specific elements that, while we may not bother to itemise them, have their own and distinct identities nevertheless.

It is only when a crisis hits and our mood drops that we may for the first time feel, with acute sorrow, what these 'reasons to live' might have been all along; it's as we lose our reasons that we understand them with uncommon clarity. We realise why we have for years bothered to rise out of bed with energy and relative good humour, put up with inconveniences, struggled to get ourselves across to others and looked forward to tomorrow – and wonder in dismay how we will ever have the will and courage to continue from now on.

Our engagement with life might have been bound up with the enjoyment of work or of reputation, the companionship of a child or of a friend, the agility of our bodies or the creativity of our minds. Denied such advantages, we don't merely miss out on an aspect of life; the whole of it loses its purpose. Secondary satisfactions – whether from a holiday or a book, a dinner with old acquaintances or a hobby – cannot compensate. The hedonic scaffolding of our lives disintegrates. We may not actively try to kill ourselves, but we can't count as quite alive either. We are going through the motions; living corpses following a script drained of meaning.

When we say that someone has fallen mentally ill, what we are frequently pointing to is the loss of long-established reasons to remain alive. The task ahead is to make a series of interventions, as imaginative as they are kind, that could return the unfortunate sufferer to a feeling of the value of their own survival.

This can never simply be a matter of telling someone in pain what the answers are or of presenting them with a ready-made checklist of options without any sincere or subtle connections with their own characters. It is at best cruel to tell an ailing person blithely to cheer up because the sun is shining and they have enough money to feed themselves; it's impossible to hector anyone back to health. If we are to recover a true taste for life, it can only be on the basis that others have been creative and accommodating enough to learn the particularities of our upsets and reversals and are armed with a sufficiently complicated grasp of how resistant our minds can be to the so-called obvious and convenient answers.

Awkwardly, perhaps, we tend not to be able to heal on our own. In situations of true despair, our ability to think disintegrates (this is in large part what mental illness is), so we need the minds of others to lend support to our native attempts to disentangle our confusions.

The process of dialogue, reflection and recuperation may be arduous, but we can hang on to one essential and cheering thought: that no life, whatever the apparent obstacles, has to be extinguished. There are invariably ways for it to be rendered liveable again; there are always reasons to be found why a person – any person – might go on. What matters is the degree of perseverance, ingenuity and love we can bring to the task of reinvention and remodelling.

Most probably, the reasons why we might end up living will look very different after the crisis compared with what they were before. Like water that has been blocked, our ambitions and enthusiasms will need to seek alternative channels down which to flow. We might not be able to put our confidence in our old social circle or occupation, our partner or our way of thinking. We will have to create new stories about who we are and what counts. We may need to forgive ourselves for errors, give up on a need to feel exceptional, surrender worldly ambitions and cease once and for all to imagine that our minds could be as logical or as reliable as we had hoped.

If there is any advantage to going through a mental crisis of the worst kind, it is that, on the other side of it, we will have ended up choosing life rather than merely assuming it to be the unremarkable norm. We, the ones who have crawled back from the darkness, may be disadvantaged in a hundred ways, but at least we will have had to find, rather than assumed or inherited, reasons why we are still here. Our satisfactions will be all the more intense and our gratitude more profound for having been consciously arrived at.

The challenge from the present sickness can be mapped out in its essential form: one day to reach a small but robust and persuasive list of reasons to continue to be.

2.
Acceptance

One of the great contributing factors to mental illness is the idea that we should be well at all costs and all times. We suffer far more than we should because of how long it can take many of us until we allow ourselves to fall properly and usefully ill.

For many years we may be able to evade our symptoms skilfully, pulling off an accomplished impression of what counts – in our unobservant societies – as a healthy human. We may gain all the accoutrements of so-called success – love, a career, family, prestige – without anyone bothering to note the sickness behind our eyes. We may take care to fill our days with activity so that we can be guaranteed to have no time to deal with any of the sores that blister inside. We can rely on the extraordinary prestige of being busy to avoid the truly hard work of doing nothing other than sitting with our minds and their complicated sorrows. When pressures build, we may develop a raft of opaque physical ailments that baffle and excite the medical profession, or we can acquire a paranoid worldview that identifies all our enemies with political and economic ideologies rather than with anything psychological closer to home.

We may be deep into midlife before the problems finally emerge with clarity. When they do, it is liable to be extremely inconvenient to those around us. We may be unable to get out of bed. We might say the same mysterious sentence again and again. We might still be in our pyjamas at midday and awake and wide-eyed at 2 a.m. We might cry at inopportune moments or shout angrily at people who had always relied on us for docility.

Kind observers will say that we have had a turn, an episode or a breakdown. More impatient ones will remark that we have gone mad. The truth is that we may be closer to sanity than we have ever been, it's just that proper self-awareness can often force us to walk through the door of seeming lunacy. Well handled, a breakdown may be a prelude to a breakthrough. In order to rebuild our lives on firmer foundations, we may have to reckon with much that has not been properly addressed since the start: an unresolved sense of unworthiness, a fury at a neglectful caregiver, a terror around our sexuality.

In a crisis, our chances of getting better rely to a significant extent on having the right relationship to our illness; an attitude that is relatively unfrightened by our distress and that isn't overly in love with the idea of always seeming 'normal', which can allow us to be unwell for a while in order one day to reach a more authentic kind of sanity.

It will help us in this quest if the images of mental illness we can draw on do not narrowly imply that our ailment is merely a pitiable possibility; if we can appeal to images that tease out

Top: Francisco Goya, *Yard with Lunatics*, 1794

Bottom: Sylvia Plath, at home, 1962

the universal and dignified themes of our state, so that we do not have to fear and hate ourselves for being unwell on top of everything else. We stand to heal much faster if there are fewer associations like those created by the Spanish painter Goya (of madness as the seventh circle of hell) and more of men and women a little like you and me, sitting on the sofa, able to combine our inner wretchedness with other, more temperate and attractive qualities – so that we remain every bit human, despite our terrifying convulsions, absences of mind, catastrophic forebodings and sense of despair.

It would help too if the places we were encouraged to visit when we were sick could have some architectural merit that would enforce an impression that illness was compatible with grace, and that by looking into our mental problems we were not at the same time cutting ourselves off from humanity but simply acceding to a denser and richer variety of it.

The best philosophical background against which to wrestle with mental unwellness is one that conceives of the human animal as intrinsically rather than accidentally flawed; a philosophy that rejects the notion that we could ever be perfect and instead welcomes our griefs and our errors, our stumbles and our follies as no less a part of us than our triumphs and our intelligence.

Tea bowl, 17th century. Life is fundamentally misshapen and imperfect, yet still dignified and graceful.

Tea bowl, White Satsuma ware with gold lacquer repairs,

Edo period, 17th century

Japan's Zen Buddhism boldly expresses such thoughts, with its declaration that life itself is suffering, and its veneration in the visual arts – and by extension in its psychology – of all that is imperfect and unglossy: rainy autumn evenings, sadness, moss-covered roofs, stained wooden panels, tears and, most famously, misshapen and irregular pieces of pottery.

Against such a background, it becomes much easier for us to accept ourselves in our unwell state. We feel less guilty that we are not at work and are not playing up to the roles demanded of us by responsible others. We can be less defensive and frightened, more inclined to seek out care and more likely to recover properly in time.

With a philosophy of acceptance in mind, we can recognise that whatever the particularities of our crisis (which will need to be investigated with time), our pains fit into a broad picture of a crisis-prone human condition. No one is spared. No life can escape significant troubles. We don't have to know the details of someone's life to be able to guess at the sort of difficulties they too will encounter. We have all been born to inadequate parents; our desires will always exceed reality; we will all make some appalling errors; we will hurt those we love and anger those with power over us; we will be anxious and confused, woeful and lost. We should accept both that we are profoundly unwell and that our ailments are entirely normal.

Japanese philosophy has another lesson for us at this point: we will probably one day be pieced back together, but we are likely to retain substantial and ineradicable scars. Yet these marks can be worn with pride and self-respect. According to Zen Buddhism's tradition of *kintsugi*, an accidentally smashed bowl is not to be thrown away in embarrassment; its fragments can be carefully collected and reassembled with glue inflected with gold. The traces of repair are made obvious, celebrated and cherished, as if to suggest to us – as we bring a cup to our lips – that we do not have to give up on ourselves or be ashamed of our own brokenness.

We can confront our illness without panic or fear, with a quiet, intelligent sadness perhaps best captured by the word 'melancholy'. If we were searching for a patron saint of such a melancholy relationship to mental difficulty, we might pick the Welsh artist Gwen John (1876–1939), who combined a career as an excellent painter with moments of mental collapse, but remained all the while fundamentally on the side of life.

From her self-portrait, John implies that she would understand whatever we might be going through. Her eyes hint that she has been there too, that she could be our guide to the underworld of our minds and that, however much we might hate ourselves at this moment, we deserve gentleness, patience and respect as we feel our way towards repair.

Gwen John, *Self Portrait*, 1902

3.
Medication

When we are physically unwell, a standard strategy is to head to the doctor, take a pill and then expect to feel a lot better in a short while. This recourse is so established, so practical and generally so successful, it is only natural if we were to try to replicate it in the mental field. Here too, when we are feeling ill, we may want to visit a doctor, take a pill and wait for our symptoms to disperse.

For most of the history of humanity, there was no medication available when one was mentally afflicted (aside from obviously fraudulent concoctions). The full force of one's sickness had to run unchecked; there would be uncontained sobbing, violence and despondency. It was said that the screams of the inmates of London's Bethlem Royal Hospital, more popularly known as Bedlam, had the power to curdle the blood of listeners a mile away. There seemed little to do with mental sufferers other than place them in cells, tie them in chains and do one's best to forget they existed.

Then, in 1950, Paul Charpentier, a French chemist working at Laboratories Rhône-Poulenc, succeeded in synthesising a drug called 4560RP, later renamed chlorpromazine. When rats were injected with it, placed in a crowded cage and convulsed with electric shocks, they showed none of the expected alarm and frenzy, settling instead into a serene and indifferent mood. When given to humans, the drug had a similar calming effect: American soldiers in the Korean War were able to walk onto the battlefield with total fearlessness. In hospitals, psychotic patients who were placed on the drug became sociable, unaggressive and ready to rejoin ordinary life.

The world's first antipsychotic drug was born. Over the coming decades, it was followed by dozens more seemingly miraculous medicines, all of them playing – in ways that their creators did not and still do not entirely understand – with the brain's receptors for dopamine, the hormone held to be responsible for excessive excitement and fear.

Alongside these antipsychotics, there emerged a family of antidepressants, in particular those known as SSRIs, that could increase the brain's levels of serotonin, the neurotransmitter and hormone associated with uplift, motivation and positive moods. The names of these drugs included fluoxetine, citalopram, paroxetine, escitalopram, risperidone, quetiapine and aripiprazole.

Modern psychiatry ended up operating with broadly two essential instruments: medication that could calm us down (reducing terror, paranoia, mania, disinhibition, insomnia and aggression) and medication that could lift us up (alleviating despair, moroseness and loss of meaning).

Thanks to these medicines, occupancy rates of psychiatric hospitals plummeted, decreasing by some 80% in developed countries between 1955 and 1990. Illnesses that had been a near-death sentence a generation before could now be managed through the use of carefully administered pills, injections or patches. It looked as if our unruly minds had finally been tamed.

But the answer was not complete. Unfortunately, a lot of medicines turned out to have physical side effects, some of which were rather serious (being intermittently responsible for dramatic weight gain, diabetes, kidney malfunction and blood clots). Yet the charge against them at a psychological level was more fundamental: that, on the basis of their approach, they did not and could never get to grips with the true causes of mental illness. At best, they could control appalling symptoms while being unable to grapple with what in the individual's past had led to them in the first place.

To be fair to psychiatry, even if this were true, it is no mean feat to be able to offer a person a measure of control over their mental symptoms, given the horrors that these can entail. Those of us who have known mental illness from close up might have, at the height of our suffering, chosen to be physically tortured rather than endure yet more of the abominations our minds can inflict.

There are varieties of mental unwellness in which we are taken over by anxiety and foreboding and paralysed by a sense that every minute is carrying us closer to an immense and unnameable catastrophe. We can no longer eat or speak; we may just have to lie in a ball crying and waiting for the axe to fall. There are states in which we wake up every morning with a conviction that we need to take an overdose in order to end the turmoil in our minds. There can be voices inside us that never cease telling us that we are guilty, shameful and abhorrent. We may live in terror that we are about to lose control or might already have done so. Our imaginations can be haunted by images of harming ourselves or others. It can feel as if there is a monster inside us urging us to do appalling deeds and filling our consciousness with lacerating persecutory thoughts. We may feel our inner coherence dissolving and giving way to a maelstrom of aggression and paranoia. We may be so mysteriously sad that no pleasantry or act of kindness can distract us; all we wish to do is stare mutely out of the window and hope to be gone soon.

With the right medication to hand, however, some of these nightmares can end. We may know our anxiety is still there, but we are granted some distance from it; we are able to stare at it as if it were an enraged tiger in a zoo on the other side of a thick pane of glass. We may not lose sight of our despair and self-loathing, but we can acquire an attitude of detachment in relation to it; it doesn't matter quite so much that we are awful and should end it all. We can park the idea for a morning in order to do some work or clean the house. We can put off thoughts of suicide until tomorrow. We don't need to have a complete reckoning with our sadistic ideas at every moment. The crushing sadness can partially lift, and we might have the energy for a conversation with a friend or a walk in the park. Only someone who hadn't endured vicious mental suffering would dare to casually dismiss such psychiatric interventions as a plaster over a wound.

Nevertheless, most mental illness has a psychological history, and its hold on us will only weaken the more episodes of this painful history we can start to feel and make sense of. Medication may be able to change the background atmosphere of our minds, but our thoughts about ourselves need to be challenged and adjusted with conscious instruments if we are to be able to grow truly well. The genuine resolution of mental disturbance lies in our ability to think, especially of our early childhoods and the key figures and events within it.

The unfortunate paradox is that illnesses of the mind generally affect precisely the instrument that we require to interpret our lives. It is our conscious reason that is both sick and desperately needed in order to do battle with despair and fear; it is reason that we need to locate persuasive grounds to keep going. This is where medication may usefully join up with psychotherapy to deliver a coherent solution. We might say that the supreme role of pills is to hold back panic and sadness in our daily lives, so we can regain some control over our mental health; they aren't in themselves the cure, but they are the essential tools that can make therapy, and through it authentic healing, possible. They promise our minds the rest and safety they require to harness their own strengths.

4.
Regulation

Efforts to re-regulate the mind so that it can reflect on, and interpret, itself do not stop at medication. If the goal is to soothe and reassure ourselves, then we can explore a number of interventions – ranging across very different fields, some of them seldom judged as belonging to mental health – to help us to rebuild and maintain our psyches. We may need to look way beyond the mind to make our minds well again.

This holistic approach is accepted in other areas of endeavour. We understand that in order to create a world-class athlete, it isn't enough to work on someone's muscle strength. We need to watch how they sleep, what they eat, the company they keep, the clothes they wear. Similar care is taken when trying to train elite soldiers or musicians; a whole way of life has to be examined and adjusted in order to deliver the right results.

The foremost example of this totalising approach can be found in the history of religions. Behind the invention of the monastery is the notion that in order to fashion a mind that can focus appropriately on the divine, many details will need to be considered and rethought: what sort of hairstyle someone has, the kind of material their tunic is made out of, what time they have breakfast, how they sit when they read or contemplate and what the view should look like out of the window.

Underpinning such interest is a conception of the human being as immensely susceptible to the influence of what we in the secular realm tend to call – with fateful neglect – 'small things'. It seldom occurs to us to trace the connection between apparently incidental sensory and physical routines and what passes through our minds. We treat the mind as a more or less isolated organ that can continue to function as we would want it whatever food we serve it, however much rest we give it and whatever architectural or natural vistas lie before its eyes.

We deem it impossible that our thoughts could be coloured by the sort of light we are exposed to, the articles we read or the kind of exercise we take. No such indifference was permitted in Zen Buddhism or Catholicism; these careful belief systems developed elaborate traditions around posture, tea drinking, breathing and gardening because they did not subscribe to our walled-off vision of the mind. They saw continuity between beliefs and – among other elements – how we bathe, the words we say on waking up, the kind of crockery we use and the speed at which we eat our dinner.

We should take inspiration from this spiritual vigilance in the quest for our own mental health. We should borrow from the manic sensitivity of religions to imagine spaces and routines that can give our minds the best possible chances of finding, and holding on to, robust reasons to keep going.

Here are some of the elements we might consider:

Sleep

Part of the reason why many of us have a tangled and unhelpful relationship with sleep can be traced back to the way we first learnt about the subject many years ago. Parents of small children tend to be very careful about bedtimes. They favour early nights; they give their babies plenty of naps throughout the day; they think a lot about blackout curtains; they are quick to diagnose many instances of bad temper as stemming from a background deficit of rest, and while they may be indulgent in some areas, they are likely to be implacable in any negotiation over routines.

None of this is altruistic: tired small children are a nightmare to look after. Every reversal becomes a drama, every disappointment turns into a catastrophe and every excitement shifts into mania. A halfway decent adult existence is impossible alongside a tired child. Self-interest necessitates totalitarianism.

But while a draconian philosophy is useful in the early years, it can set up an awkward dynamic in a child's mind as adolescence sets in. Growing up and asserting one's independence and individuality can then become associated with a newly defiant and cavalier approach to bedtimes. The strictures and denying rules of the past are not for a newly empowered young adult.

Why bother to put the light out by ten or even midnight or one in the morning, given that one is so obviously no longer a toddler? Given that one has no more use for nappies, why would one need to worry that one was still finishing something on the computer as the first signs of dawn appeared in the eastern sky?

What is thereby missed is how much every adult shares in a young child's sensitivity to a shortfall of sleep. Just like our younger selves, we do not have a reasonable view of our own prospects or condition. There are many different ways of telling the story of our lives, ranging from an optimistic tale of progress mixed with noble defeats to a tragic narrative of thoroughgoing stupidity and unforgivable errors. What can determine the difference between madness and sanity may be nothing grander, but then again nothing more critical, than how long our minds have been allowed to rest in the preceding hours.

It's unfortunate that this connection is so easy to miss. No bells go off in our minds warning us that we are running low on nocturnal nectar; there are probably no parents around any more to nag us up to our rooms; plenty of well-meaning friends will invite us out for evenings that begin at 9 p.m.; our screens never fail to have something new and interesting to tell us at every hour – and no stylish or authoritative figures in the public realm ever seem to urge us to turn in early or proudly show off their cautious bedtime routines. Being meticulous about sleep seems like something only a very dull or defeated person would care about.

As a result, we start to believe many dark things with doomful ease: that our relationship is over, that everyone hates us, that our lives are meaningless and that human existence is a cosmic joke. 'When we are tired, we are attacked by ideas we conquered long ago,' knew Friedrich Nietzsche. We go mad from tiredness long before we notice the role that exhaustion is playing in stealing our sanity.

We need to recover some of the wisdom of our early years. We may be a sizeable height, holding down an important job and capable of making impressive moves, but where it counts in our resilience to emotional chaos, we are no more robust than a very young infant. Whenever we sense our spirits sinking and folly and anxiety pressing in on us, we should abandon all endeavours and head to the bedroom. We should be as proud of our regimented sleep patterns as we are about a neat house or a flourishing career.

Underpinning our care should be modesty. While thinking through our problems is crucial to our health, to attempt to think without enough sleep is worse than not thinking at all. The thinking we do when tired is vindictive and sloppy. It misses important details; it gives the advantage over to our enemies; it hands victory to the evangelists of sadness. It isn't a disrespect to the power of the mind to insist that we should not attempt to fire up this machine unless and until it has been adequately well rested – like a powerful rocket or an exquisite motorboat that one wouldn't dare to activate unless we could be sure of a clear sky or a calm sea.

Understanding our vulnerability, we should never take seriously any worry that suddenly appears extremely pressing after ten in the evening. What we panic about in the early hours should automatically be discounted. No large conversation or argument should ever be undertaken past 9 p.m.

Being careful doesn't just apply to the night. At varied points in the day, when we are overwhelmed, we should know to stop and hoist a white flag. It may look as if we should keep trying to fight our demons. In fact, we need to elude them with a nap. We may feel guilty, but it is more irresponsible to try to keep going than it is to know that the game is up for now. There is never anything shameful in admitting one can't cope. It's this knowledge that guarantees us a chance to fight another round soon.

When we lie in bed, it makes sense to think of ourselves as akin to a smaller, furry mammal: a rabbit or perhaps a squirrel. We should lift our knees up very close to our chests and pull the duvet over our heads. We might soak a whole patch of the pillow with our tears. We should – metaphorically – stroke our own weary foreheads as a loving adult might once have done for us when we were a child. Grown-up life is intolerably hard, and we should be allowed to know and lament this.

We shouldn't feel weird in our weepy squirrel position. Other people go to immense lengths to hide that they do, or would like to do, the very same sort of thing. We need to know someone extremely well – better than we know 99% of humanity – before they will let us in on the scale of their despair and anxiety and their longings for a cosy, safe nook. It looks child-like, but it is in fact the essence of adulthood to recognise, and give space for, one's regressive tendencies.

What the curled squirrel position indicates is that not all mental problems can be solved by active reasoning. Not thinking consciously should also be deemed a part of the mind's work. Being curled up in bed allows our minds to do a different sort of thinking, the sort that can take place when we are no longer impatiently looking for results, when the usual hectoring conscious self takes a break and lets the mind do what it will for a time. It is then, paradoxically, that certain richer, more creative ideas can have the peace and freedom to coalesce – as they may do when we are out for a walk or idling in a café. Thinking isn't what we do best when it's all we're meant to do.

There remain plenty of reasons to enjoy life. We simply may not be able to see them until we have allowed ourselves the privilege of a weepy nap or a long night's sleep.

Food

Mental illness is often bound up with a sense of shame, self-disgust and self-flagellation. We scour our past for reasons to hate who we are. We appear in our own eyes as unworthy and despicable candidates who should never have been allowed to be.

It's a measure of the close connection between diet and mental health that such thoughts are particularly likely to come to the fore following certain sorts of meals. After a lunch or dinner soaked in trans-fat and sodium nitrate, processed sugar and corn syrup, saccharin and palm oil, potassium benzoate and butylated hydroxyanisole, reasons for our nonexistence can appear especially persuasive.

In a quest for mental health, we would be advised to take in more ingredients that help to dampen our anxiety, weaken our self-hatred and strengthen our sense of hope. Some of the following are especially recommended in a diet for a vulnerable mind:

Chamomile tea
We, the ones forever on the edge of being overwhelmed, hardly require anything to stimulate us any further. We have vivid

thoughts aplenty without the fluorescent colours added by caffeine or alcohol. What we require above all is something that can slow our racing thoughts and hold us to our most sensible and quiet mental pathways. With a cup full of hot chamomile tea, we will be forced to sip slowly, the steam will gently caress our eyelids and we will treat ourselves as who we really are, without any pejorative connotations: convalescents.

Figs

We should incline to foods that have been tampered with as little as possible by the artifice and wiliness of chemists – and that would have been around in much the same form when the world still had some of its original innocence and quiet. The fig seems to understand sadness and vulnerability. It keeps its appeal muted. It may not be until after we have eaten one that we properly appreciate how nourishing and flavourful it was beneath its serene, unshowy exterior. It urges us to follow it in its attitude of humility and reticence.

Nuts

Especially sympathetic to mental health are handfuls of walnuts and hazelnuts, cashew nuts and (unsalted) pistachios. They seem to rein in the ambitions that ordinarily torture us; they satisfy us with little and thereby urge us to quieten our restlessness and ignore the chatter and excitement of the public square. They reach a special pitch of their sanity-inducing goodness when accompanied by three or four dried apricots.

Dates
A good life can't be free of moments of delight and ecstasy, and the date knows this. There has to be a place for a degree of excitement. The date delivers ravishment when required, but it is also limited in its power to derail us. It will never render us manic. We could not – even though it can seem as though we might – become addicts of this fruit. It won't allow us to escape ourselves for too long, but it will, for a few moments at least, re-orient us towards the light.

Feta cheese, Kalamata olives, bread
This should count as a meal for us in moods of mental torment, taking us back to a basic existence and reassuring us that this can be tolerable and wholesome. We don't need very much to survive. The walls may have closed in, yet pleasure can be drawn from the most apparently insignificant elements. We may lose everything, but there will still be this and, alongside it, the love and care of a few imaginative and loyal people.

Dark chocolate
It can be as black as the night we fear, but it is – without melodramatic sweetness and with a grown-up, understanding sternness – on our side. It leaves behind an almost metallic

taste that endows us with courage and resolve without adding guilt or judgement.

In our ill moods we're unlikely to have the energy to cook or think of food, so we can end up vulnerable to the blandishments of processed dishes. Yet we should take care that food never becomes yet another reason why we might hate or regret ourselves. We should lean on a few simple menu ideas to carry us across the most difficult, frightened phases of our inner lives:

Menu ideas for the mentally fragile

Breakfast	Lunch	Dinner
Two figs, a cupful of blueberries, five walnuts, Greek yoghurt	Canned tuna in olive oil, artichoke hearts, sundried tomatoes	Scrambled eggs on rye bread, grilled mushrooms, wilted spinach
Two dates, a banana, porridge	Avocado on toast, topped with toasted seeds	Salmon escalope, broccoli, French beans
Orange and lime juice, granola with almond milk	Feta, olives, bread	Scallops, wild rice, lentils

Bathing

It is a sign of our lack of civilisation that we insist on thinking of baths primarily as tools to clean ourselves with, rather than honouring them as what they truly are: instruments of mental health.

The Romans would have been astonished by our modern plumbing: our ability to summon up a flawless cauldron of piping hot water at the turn of a tap inside almost every home at negligible cost. Our boilers would have awed them, our pipework would have been the envy of their engineers. These were people who did not consider a country or province properly colonised until public baths had been constructed, who moved mountains and cut through forests to ensure a regular supply of hot water, who left behind elegant bathing establishments from Northern England to the edges of the Sahara Desert, from Merida in the Iberian West to Palmyra in the Levantine East.

Yet it would have puzzled the Romans how silent we are on the deeper resonances of bathing, how few poems and odes there are to our moments in the tub, how unimaginative we tend to be about the powers of hot water to heal our souls.

All of us have come from warm, watery encasements and, when mental troubles strike, we should immediately head back into the bath to be held, as the womb once did, in a tight aquatic embrace.

Hot water is a symbol of love and care. It allows us to let down our guard. We can – as at so few other moments – be at once defenceless and safe, naked yet cosy. We can bolt the door, turn down the lights and allow ourselves to do nothing for a time other than watch the water lap our knees and occasionally top up the temperature with a small scalding infusion.

We don't need to force ourselves to arrive at any great conclusions. This is a time to idle and free associate. We can let the mind wander, perhaps backwards to more innocent days or to the moment when the troubles began. We can float over our lives without our usual critical inclinations. We can drown our pain in the heat, we can cauterise our mental wounds, our tears can lose themselves in the steam.

We may want to keep a small towel and a pad of paper and a pencil by the bath, in case something strikes us that could put a better spin on our travails. Or we can simply float and wait for some of the panic to subside, as it surely will.

Those of us who suffer in our minds should not be embarrassed to have multiple baths a day. They will be the enamel ships that carry us over the worst of our griefs.

Exercise

One of the great impediments to taking exercise is the idea that being unwilling to do so is caused first and foremost by 'laziness'. The reason why we are sitting on the sofa a lot, or spending considerable time in bed, or are seriously reluctant to run is that we are – in essence – bone idle.

But we must get to the root of what is really going on with the mentally unwell: we don't sit around because we are lazy; we do so because we are ill. It is a specific feature of mental illness that one may be especially hampered when it comes to moving one's body with any degree of vigour.

One might say that mental illness makes one retreat. From the world in general, its trees, its people, its sagas and concerns and joys. But it also makes one retreat from one's own body, from its limbs, its skin and its right to be. One might say that illness squats at the front of consciousness in pain and is reluctant for anything carefree or mobile or fluid to get through.

Many varieties of mental illness freeze us – not with fear, necessarily, though that too – but with self-hatred, shame, anxiety and regret. With such moods coursing through us, we are in no easy position to stretch, to run or to gambol. We are rooted to our spot, a place of sadness, misery and dread.

We know all the arguments in favour of exercise – they are incontestable. Our limbs need to move, our lungs need rapid oxygenation, our skin needs to sweat vigorously. But when we are ill, these arguments end up feeling punitive and accusatory.

They remind us of all that we are incapable of, of how badly we have failed and of how awful we are.

To have any chance of exercising, we need a different, more forgiving approach. Firstly, one built on a lot of modesty. One is ill and one can't be an athlete, certainly not for now. So, by 'exercise', one is going to have to mean something far gentler than might ideally be recommended. Realistically, it's going to mean going for a walk and not much more. It doesn't sound like any sort of feat, but nor do many of the achievements of those who are in recovery; they seem heroic only once one knows what the individual has to go through to pull them off.

The walk might be once around the block – or twice. But it will be extremely valuable, especially if it is repeated every day. In many forms of mental illness, such is one's degree of shame, one doesn't feel one has permission to leave the house. One feels it is illegitimate to be outside 'enjoying oneself'; one feels one will be seen and negatively judged. One wants to hide and feels like a monster in the eyes of others. So, it's an enormous feat to put on a coat and, against all one's instincts, wander out as though the world could be a habitable, welcoming and safe place.

Yet how salutary it can be to take the risk, because there is healing to be found in the sight of the trees on the horizon, the starlings in a hedge, a duck by the meadow, a dog next to the supermarket. What we are seeing is soothing evidence that the world exists beyond our own cruel, mean-spirited, ill minds. There is so much that knows nothing of us, that is gloriously indifferent (those stars appearing in the dusk sky) and that isn't there to shame us. We slowly re-inhabit our own bodies.

Outside seems so much more normal than what is inside our heads. We can take inspiration: someone is moving house, a child is playing with a stick, there is a cat on a wall resting in the sun. Things may not be as awful as we had assumed, when it was just us in our bedroom, going through the narrow, dark corridors of memory. We can feel our feet taking slightly longer steps, our lungs working a little more actively. We have walked once around the block already and no one has attacked us, no one has mocked us, no one is laughing. We are doing extremely well.

We shouldn't push it; exercise can be very minor and still wholly beneficial. We aren't going to be marathon runners, but we have managed something extraordinary nevertheless. We're athletes of a different sort, tackling a different enemy, and our battle is already well under way.

Silence

The news media serves two essential constituencies: people who are running nations and businesses; and people whose lives are a little too quiet, a little too undramatic and a little too serene for their own tastes.

These two broad categories are unlikely to comprise anyone who self-identifies as mentally unwell. The last thing that we need when things are going awry in our minds is yet more evidence of folly, melodrama, chaos, aggression, partisanship and an absence of forgiveness. We owe it to ourselves to become willingly more ignorant of what is going on in our highly disturbed and disturbing media.

The minds of the mentally ill are already engaged in titanic struggles and battles: while there may be no outward movement, inside there will be gargantuan attempts to answer back against the monsters of self-hatred and to hold back the door against the hounds of self-contempt. One will be facing flood waters of anxiety that try to sweep away every last hope in their path, crushing like toys elements one had placed in their way, like plans and affiliations and a sense of identity. If one could hear some of this struggle, it would have some of the melodramatic sounds of a Wagner opera; if one could see it, it would have the turbulent quality of a Turner painting. Someone could be sitting down on the sofa, looking sad, occasionally putting a finger to their lips, while inside their benighted mind, scenes might be unfolding akin to *Valley of Aosta: Snowstorm, Avalanche, and Thunderstorm* set to the sounds of 'The Ride of the Valkyries'.

Joseph Mallord William Turner, *Valley of Aosta: Snowstorm, Avalanche, and Thunderstorm*, c. 1836–1837

In the circumstances, one doesn't need to have one's nerve endings further shocked and titillated. What one urgently needs is quiet. Despite the pressure to 'stay informed' and know 'what is going on', one's real responsibilities lie elsewhere – in not knowing a great many things in order that one can keep faith with life itself. One will have one's hands full reviewing one's past, battling despair and hanging on to reasons why it might be worth surviving until next summer. This leaves no time to be curious about the parliamentary elections or the latest dilemmas facing an actor and her partner. The apparently innocent activity of reading the headlines now counts as hugely reckless.

We should tell those who love us and are living in our vicinity to help us direct our minds towards hope and kindness. We should beg them to switch off all social media and not bring any papers into the house. Let them not refer to anything that hasn't been around for 200 years at least; we should focus on eternal verities and on small, sympathetic, generous ideas near to home.

We need serenity in which to challenge our beliefs that we are awful, that the worst will happen to us and that we won't be able to survive. We need calm in which to rebuild faith in ourselves and existence more broadly. To assist us, we need interiors like those depicted in the work of the great Norwegian master of stillness, Vilhelm Hammershøi; rooms in which the sun washes onto clean, empty surfaces and all one can hear in

Vilhelm Hammershøi, *Interior in Strandgade, Sunlight on the Floor*, 1901

the distance might be the sounds of a child playing in the yard or some pigeons on the roof opposite.

We don't need any further arguments in favour of chaos and nastiness. We have plenty of this in our heads for twelve lifetimes. We don't need to titillate ourselves with the thought that the world might run out of oil or be rocked by a nuclear accident or that a new disease might ravage us. Let someone else keep an eye on the bigger picture; call us only when the crisis is at the door. For now, leave us to fight our inner world-shaking struggles in a corner of a quiet, sunlit room.

Architecture

It would be so convenient and so much cheaper if our mental health had no relationship whatsoever to architecture. We could make ourselves happily at home in almost any environment and not suffer in the least. But the reality is that we are open to the suggestions embedded in three-dimensional space, especially when these urge us towards despair and make covert arguments for the meanness and hopelessness of our condition.

We need beauty not out of greed or because we are effete or difficult but because we are ill. What we mean by beauty is environments that speak, in the idiom of paint, fabric, wood and glass, about such themes as sanity and sweetness and hope, all of which we desperately need to know a lot more about.

John Pawson, The Life House, Wales, 2016.

A room for a convalescent.

It's because we are unwell that we need to grow interested in interior decoration. We need places where an inspiring style marries up simplicity with dignity; we need care to have been taken with floorboards and skirtings. Someone needs to have approached the crockery with love and embedded tenderness in the choice of cushions and curtains. We need repose and softness – and small vestiges of hope and enchantment, cosiness and concern.

This psychological palette might translate into such elements as limestone walls, delicate window frames, fresh white paint with creamy tones, jars with daffodils or violets in them, rich woollen blankets; we might end up in a sober, monk-like cell enlivened by touches of goodwill.

If the budget allowed, we might go and live in a monastery for the mind, with exquisite bedrooms off a central atrium, gardens of lemon and orange trees, covered walkways, fountains, gravel paths and cypresses. We aren't being aesthetically fussy with such daydreams; we're getting interested in architecture because we're trying to get well again.

Household tasks

The traditional approach to mental healing stresses the need to face up to our demons, at all times and with full courage. The underlying idea is that we fall ill when we attempt to back away from certain painful but necessary truths about our inner lives: that we are in an unhappy relationship, that we were traumatised in childhood, that we are addicted to a substance or have not dared to do justice to our sexuality. We will only get well – so the theory goes – once we cease to crowd out our own reality; the glare of honesty will save us.

But while we can recognise the toll of certain forms of denial, we can still make a nuanced case for the other side, for the occasional need – especially when we are very unwell – to take some time off from self-analysis. We should do so not in a spirit of escape, but rather from a feeling of consciously giving ourselves a few hours away from our problems so that we can return to ourselves with renewed creativity and strength. Distraction intelligently handled can be a part of mental healing.

We might therefore want to recommend that the mentally fragile make soup or freeze batches of pasta sauces; weed the garden and seed flowers for the spring; scour the internet for new kinds of peripherals for the computer; ensure that the stairs are spotless and the windows free of all finger marks or invest in a strange kind of sanding machine with which finally to sort out the damp patch on the skirting by the shower.

Of course, it's important to talk about key figures of childhood and to try to trace the origins of our fears of disgrace. But it could be as important, at other moments, to run away from the incessant pain inside us by making fishcakes and raking the garden.

Small household tasks offer us a metaphor for the sort of fixing we're interested in, but can't yet quite manage, inside ourselves. They give us the courage to imagine a day when we might be as tidy inside of our minds as the linen cupboard presently is on the outside.

There is kindness in making sure a mentally unwell person has a few untaxing duties to take care of every day. Monasteries understood the unruliness of the mind and the kindly role of chores in assuaging it. They allowed the monks to think head on of God and their responsibilities within a spiritual life for many hours at a time. But they also gave them moments to think of something that was simpler and more exhausting, that offered domestic paradise as a goad to picturing its grander, heavenly version. Hence the emphasis on the salvation to be found out in a vegetable garden and in a kitchen, in a laundry room and in a newly dusted corridor.

It can be the height of generosity to ask someone who isn't well to help us change the sheets and prune the artichokes. It won't be work; it is in reality a minor holiday from the exhausting labours that must soon resume within.

The window of tolerance

When we think of what it means to feel mentally well, we often picture exuberance or excitement. But what really defines our optimal moments is that they are ones in which we feel *stable* – that is, to take things in our stride and to be neither weary nor fearful, bored nor manic. The goal of psychological life could be said to be stability.

It's unfortunate, therefore, how rarely we pay close attention to our levels of stability. We seldom directly interrogate ourselves as to the steadiness of our state of mind. Instead we allow our moods to yo-yo and veer, swinging between extremes without studying what activities, people, places and thoughts have the power to push us beyond our limits.

It is in this context that we might lean on one of the most useful and simple concepts in modern psychology, the idea of *the window of tolerance*. This proposes that all of us have parameters within which we can operate comfortably, with a sense of competence and security, adequacy and spiritedness. Challenges may come our way, but we can engage with them collectedly; they aren't going to be the end of us and everything we care for. We might feel tired, but we know how to offer ourselves the rest and calm we require to recover. Something or someone is proving very frustrating, but we don't veer into rage animated by a terror that everything is falling apart.

We can pull a wry smile and forge on. We are under pressure, but we don't have an impression of being persecuted. There's some gossip circulating about us, but we'll get on top of it mentally and find strategies to cope. We'd like to have achieved more, but we aren't going to tear ourselves apart. We might be in high spirits, but we don't slip over into risky ebullience. Our moods are ebbing and flowing within a sustainable range. We are – as the psychologists would say – living safely within our window of tolerance.

We could picture a dial within the dashboard of our minds a little like an airplane's altitude indicator, where our mood moves up and down between two lines indicating our safe parameters. Above the top line lies everything that feels *overwhelming*: this is where we slip into terror, hypervigilance, mania, guilt or shame. Below the bottom line lies everything that renders us uncomfortably *numb*: states of debilitating loneliness, boredom, deadness and alienation.

If we are fortunate, our moods will deflect sustainably between the two lines, sometimes coming a little close to overwhelming, sometimes near to numbness, but always remaining within a harmonious window. But for many of us, one way to conceive of our troubles is that we are continually, in one way or another, smashing through the mental window without even being aware of the zigzagging involved. The morning might start well, but by midday, something has triggered a breach

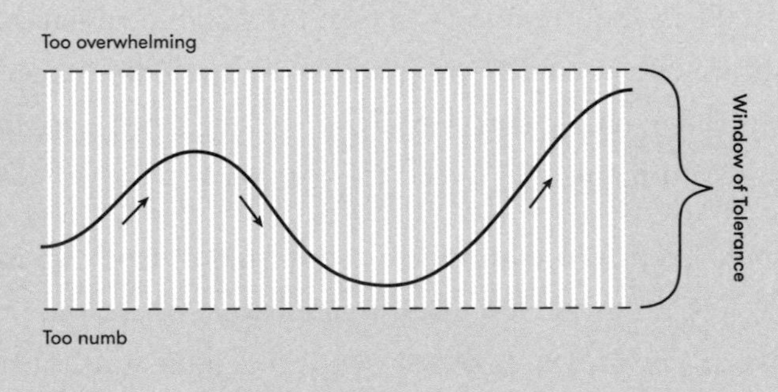
Too overwhelming
Window of Tolerance
Too numb

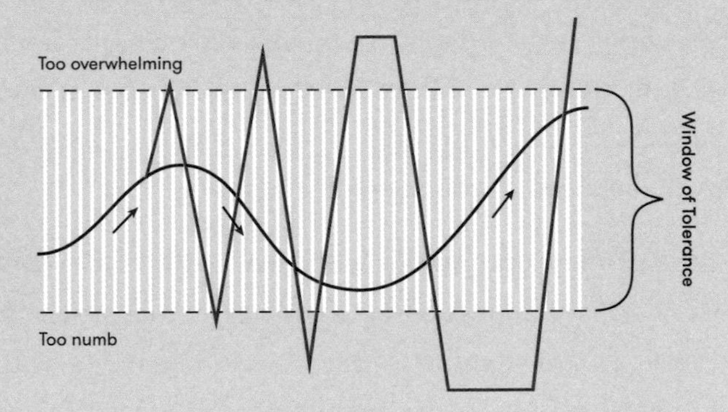
Too overwhelming
Window of Tolerance
Too numb

and we are soon in a zone of high anxiety and self-persecution, which is then followed, a few hours later, by mute sensations of loneliness and despair. We feel tossed from one extreme to another. Life is an uncomfortable storm.

Remaining within our window of tolerance is a skill. Those of us who find it easy to be there probably learnt the art of self-regulation in childhood, by having been closely coached by a loving adult. This person (who would themselves know how to remain within their window) will have been on hand at moments when we felt terrified and would have known how to make the world feel manageable again. We would have trusted them, and they would have helped us to deal with incipient feelings of shame or guilt. They would have sensed when it was getting too much and we were exhausted or needed to be held calmly for a while. Likewise, they would have picked up on our feelings of numbness when suppressed anger or self-hatred were blocking our ability to be authentic and purposeful.

Luckily, even if we lacked such a person, the skill can be learnt. The first step is to get a picture of the window of tolerance in our minds and to develop the habit of looking at it constantly, much as a good pilot will keep their altitude indicator always in view. We should learn to determine at all points of the day what sort of direction our mood is heading in. When we sense that we are on an overly aggressive trajectory towards the top or bottom borders, we should take light evasive action, as though we were playing a kind of psychological video game.

For this manoeuvre, we need to start to notice what in our way of life threatens to send us out of the window of tolerance, and everything that we know can bring us back into it. Through a lot of self-observation and introspection, we might realise, for example, that spending too much time on social media, seeing a competitive acquaintance, visiting a demanding family member, dating new people, attending parties, drinking, watching pornography or interacting with a certain colleague are all at risk of sending us beyond our window, and should therefore be undertaken only with the greatest care and in limited doses.

At the same time, we should observe and cultivate everything with the power to bring us back into our window: long, hot baths, early bedtimes, sexual moderation, reading history books, astronomy, conversations with a therapist, walks in nature, light meals, Stoic philosophy, a lot of time on our own with a diary and a trusted kind friend who knows about suffering. Remaining vigilant about our course through the window of tolerance might require us to be rather firm with ourselves and others. At points, we might need to moderate our people-pleasing impulses in the name of saving our own minds.

We might also start to tune into the windows of tolerance of those around us. We might stop trying to have certain difficult conversations with them when they are obviously far too in breach of their limits to listen to us. We might feel more compassion for people who aren't simply 'evil' or 'mad' but are temporarily, for reasons we can guess at, operating in the far extremes of their windows of tolerance. We need to keep this dial on the emotional dashboard of humanity always in our sights and do everything we can to stay within its safe parameters.

Mental convalescence

It's one of the benefits of most physical illnesses that they are immediately observable and hence command respect and kindness from those around us. We know to prop a pillow beneath the person with a broken arm; we immediately open the door to someone on crutches.

But without anyone meaning to be thoughtless, it is harder to keep this caring attitude in mind when dealing with a mentally unwell person. As sufferers, we may ourselves forget our condition and therefore launch into tasks and situations for which we are not ready, and that will undermine our efforts at recovery.

To feel well, we need to recognise fully that we are ill, and therefore that we must endure a (potentially very lengthy) period of convalescence. This will mean rigidly patrolled and regulated routines, an absence of stimulation, a huge emphasis on rest and a close monitoring of visitors. We should be as careful with ourselves as we might be if we were recovering from cancer or a lung operation. We may have no physical scars, but we should do ourselves the kindness of accepting that we are as sick as those in intensive care wards or those for whom sirens wail across the city at night.

We need to be selfish about the state of our spirits, and ruthless in removing ourselves from situations that sap us. We should go to bed early, eat lightly, bathe often, go for a walk every day, have something pleasant to distract us – and, most of all, be kind to ourselves for the mess we are in.

We should learn from physical rehabilitation how long it might take to feel well again. Recovery from a broken wrist might take six months, and it can be a year before a new hip is functioning once more. A mind that's broken can take longer still; it could be one or two years, even four or five. We shouldn't be surprised; the mind is a far more complex organ than any bone or muscle and so warrants a correspondingly lengthy period of recuperation. Nor should we expect progress to be linear. There will be many days when we will go backwards, when we'll be catapulted back into a sort of despair we had hoped to leave behind forever. We should not be discouraged; what matters is the overall trend as measured over months, not a bad day here or there. There will be periods of darkness just when we had started to hope once more, and we should greet them without panic.

We have become experts over many years in a distinct language – a language of illness and self-torture. It will take a great deal of time to unlearn it and become fluent in the language of generosity and self-compassion.

We may not formally be in any institution, but we should live with as much care and seriousness as if we were in one. We should construct hospitals for the mind in our own homes, and educate those around us about our needs. We will gradually grow well again as we learn to lead the peaceful, warm-hearted, kindly and well-regulated lives that our minds have craved for so long.

5.
Love

The one ingredient on which any recovery from serious mental illness depends is also one that, curiously and grievously, never appears in any medical handbook or psychiatric diagnostic – namely, love. The word is so fatefully associated with romance and sentimentality that we overlook its critical role in helping us to keep faith with life at times of overwhelming psychological confusion and sorrow. Love – whether from a friend, a partner, an offspring, a parent – has an indomitable power which can give us the strength to recover.

We might even say that anyone who has ever suffered from mental illness and who recovers will do so because of an experience of love, whether they consciously realise it or not. By extension, no one has ever fallen gravely mentally ill without – somewhere along the line – having suffered from a severe deficit of love. Love turns out to be the guiding strand running through the onset of, and recovery from, our worst episodes of mental unwellness.

What, then, do we mean by love, in its life-giving, mind-healing sense?

Unconditional approval

What frequently assails and derails us when we are sick in our minds is a continuous punishing sense of how terrible we are. We are lacerated by self-hatred. Without any external prompting, we think of ourselves as some of the worst people around, even the worst person on earth. Our own charge sheet against us is definitive: we are 'awful', 'terrible', 'nasty', 'bad'. We can't really say much more – and efforts to get us to expand in rational terms may run aground. We often can't even point to a specific crime. If we do, it doesn't seem to onlookers to merit quite the pitiless opprobrium we devote to it. In our illness, a primal self-suspicion bursts through our defences and overtakes our faculties, leaving no room for gentleness. We are implacably appalled by, and unforgiving of, who we are.

In such agony, a loving companion can make the difference between suicide and keeping going. Such companions do not try to persuade us of our worth head on and with cold reason; nor do they go in for showy displays of affection. They can demonstrate that we matter to them in a thousand surreptitious yet fundamental ways. They check in on us day after day; they make pleasant conversation about something that won't make us anxious; they've remembered a favourite book or a drink; they know how to make a few jokes when these help and suggest we should get some rest when they feel us drifting away.

They have a good handle on the sources of our pain, but they don't push us for a big conversation or confession. They can tolerate how ill we are and will stick by us however long it takes. We don't have to impress them; they won't worry too much about how scary we are looking and the weird things we might say. They're not going to give up on us; they're not going anywhere. We can call them at strange hours. We can sob or we can sound very adult and reasonable. They seem – remarkably – to love us in and of ourselves, for who we are rather than anything we do. They hold a loving mirror to us and help us to tolerate the reflection. It's pretty much the most beautiful and useful thing in the universe.

Non-judgement

Part of what can make the attentions of others oppressive is the note of patronising pity we detect beneath their apparent kindness. They – the well ones – have come to see us in order to help, but we sense how much they cling to a fundamental difference between the mess we are in and who they think they are. We are the unwell ones, while they will always fly the flags of health and balance. They feel sorry for us from afar. We are the proverbial drowning man and they the observer on dry land.

Loving companions bear no such hints of superiority. They do not judge us as beneath them when we lie crumpled in our pyjamas at midday, because they do not fundamentally see themselves as 'above' someone who has fallen through the floor of sanity. We may happen to be very ill at the moment, but it might as well have been them, were it not for the accidents of psychology and of neurochemistry. They don't oppress us by covertly clinging to their belief in their own inviolable solidity and competence. They throw in little sentences that indicate that they too find life very taxing, that they too are very strange and that they too might one day be in our place.

Loyalty

At the heart of many mental traumas is an early experience of abandonment. Someone, when we badly needed them, was not present – and their neglect has thrown us off balance ever since. We may find it hard to depend on others in grown-up life and lack faith that someone won't run away, or take advantage of us, in turn.

A loving companion intuits this about us, and is ready to fight to earn our trust. They know that they cannot blithely assert their loyalty, they will have to prove it, which means not deserting us at moments when others would be tempted to give up. We may try to incite despair and frustration in them as a way of testing the relationship; we may say some awful things and pretend to be indifferent. But if the companion is wise, they will listen and remain unruffled, not because they are weak, but because they understand that a basic piece of repair work around trust is under way.

We have to be given a chance – which we may have missed out on in childhood – to be a bit more demanding than usual in order to witness conclusively that this isn't enough to destroy love. We can be unwell and still acceptable to another person. How much more real love will feel once it has been shaken by our illness – and survived.

Reassurance

The future for a mentally ill person is a source of ongoing and limitless torment. A thousand questions hover: What if someone gets very angry with them? What if someone wants to take them away? What if someone tries to kill them? What if the voices in their head never go away?

The loving companion does their best to quieten the panic, by presenting the future as unknowable in its precise details but fundamentally safe and bearable. They hold open options: it will always be possible to leave town, to live quietly in a small cottage, to be at home and lead a domestic existence. No one expects them to perform great feats any more; just being is enough. There doesn't have to be pressure to earn money, to impress strangers or to be heroic. Surviving is all that matters.

More importantly, the loving companion insists that they will be there to personally ensure that the future will be manageable. When it gets terrible, they can be in each other's presence and hold each other's spirits.

The loving companion doesn't get bored of instilling the same fundamental message: I am here for you and it will be OK. Even if this OK isn't what one would ideally want, still it will be OK, better than death – which probably remains the alternative in the sufferer's mind. Quite how the years ahead are going to pan out can't be determined yet, but what is known already is that the future won't need to be unendurable, for a basic reason: because there is love.

Patience

When we are mentally ill, we are often tedious in relation to the number of anxieties we go through with others. We may want to return repeatedly to the subject of whether or not we said something terrible to someone at a party hosted by our workplace seven years ago. Or whether we might have unwittingly upset a sexual companion five years before. Or if we might go bankrupt because we didn't warn our accountant of a small move in our tax affairs.

Loving parents know that the minds of little children are comparably filled with anxiety-inducing and sometimes peculiar questions: Is there a tiger under the bed? What happens if one of the trees comes into the room and takes me away? What if someone laughs at me at school?

The temptation can be to rush and give an answer full of blustering, impatient confidence. Of course it will be fine! Nonsense, there's no tiger! And so on. But the properly loving response is to take the worry as seriously as its progenitor does and address it head on, without scoffing or denying the scale of the concern. We might get out a pad of paper and a pen and run through all the many anxieties. It doesn't matter if this is the first or the fifteenth time we have done so. Love gives us the patience to enter imaginatively into the other's worried mind and try to settle it by sensible examination of what there might be to fear.

We may be called upon to kill imaginary tigers night after night – and, on the floor with a torch, should always be ready to go through the many reasons why these big cats have – after all – decided to leave us in peace.

Just the way you are

Many mentally ill individuals have suffered all their lives from a feeling that they are not, in and of themselves, good enough. Some may have become extremely high achievers, and have worked hard for decades, in order to prove to someone who was sceptical about them at the outset that they are respectable and worthy after all. They may have craved money and status and power to shore up a ghastly feeling of not being able to matter to people unless they had first attracted society's baubles and prizes.

When they break down, what remains unbelievable to these exhausted warriors is that they could ever be loved outside of their performance in the worldly race. Surely it is only their earning potential that counts? Surely it has to be their popularity that matters?

But now that they are ill and without any of the usual tools to impress, the mentally unwell stand to discover a more complex and salutary lesson. According to the values they have been subsisting on, they are a disgrace and should kill themselves. But with any luck, in the presence of a loving companion, they can start to believe in something far more nuanced and miraculous: that they could be loved without prizes, that true love isn't about impressing or intimidating someone, that an adult can love another adult a little like a good parent loves their child – not because of anything they have done, but simply and poignantly just because they exist.

Independence of mind

A good loving companion looking after a mentally sick friend heals through their power not to care very much about 'what other people think'. Of course, out there, some people are sniggering. Of course, out there, some people judge and say that the illness isn't legitimate, or that it's deserved and that the sufferer was awful to begin with. The good companion knows enough about the perversities of the human mind not to mind when they encounter everyday prejudice and meanness; daftness is to be expected.

The hasty judgements of thousands of people will, of course, be askew and lacking proper understanding. But that is no reason to panic or give up one's original analysis. Let them laugh, let them be superior, let the idiots be idiots – such are the consoling messages of love that we need to hear when we are defenceless before the judgements of a mean world. Our loving companion knows where their loyalties lie; they won't give up on us because a mob is jeering. They aren't democrats when it comes to love. They don't care if they are in a minority of one in cherishing us.

Parental repair

Both we and our carer may be deep into adulthood, but if their tenderness heals us, it is likely to be because they are repairing a deficit of early love through their ministration. They will be reparenting our broken child selves.

One of the eternally paradoxical things about babies and small children is that they need love as much as they need milk and warmth in order to develop properly. They need to be cuddled, spoken and sung to, played with, held closely and looked at with enthusiasm. Every child needs to experience what one could term 'primary parental delight', a basic feeling that they are limitlessly wanted by those who care for them and are capable of generating intense pleasure through their very being. Without this, a child might survive, but it may struggle to thrive. Their ability to walk the earth freely will always be somewhat in doubt. They may grow up with a sense of being superfluous, disruptive and, at core, unappealing and shameful.

Such emotions feed directly into a broad range of mental illnesses – chronic anxiety, self-harm, suicidal ideation, depression – that all have roots in a sense of not having mattered enough to anyone over long childhood years.

This defines the challenge for the carer in adulthood. Some of the work will have to involve making good failures of early provision; they will need to convince the wounded inner child that what they didn't receive decades ago could still be available today; that there might still be joy, reassurance, play and kindness.

It could seem highly patronising to tell an adult that they need above all to be reparented. It's in fact the height of maturity to recognise that, if we're ever to get better, the small version of us must allow ourselves another chance to experience what it could feel like to matter limitlessly to a kindly companion.

The night

Way back, the night was the time when we were especially afraid, and especially needed love and reassurance. The same will be true in our periods of acute mental illness. The night will terrify us, stretching out as a vast and threatening space in which our worst fears and most critical voices will have unlimited dominion.

We need someone who can help us during these tortuous hours, perhaps by remaining awake next to us, or by sleeping in an adjoining bed or room or by giving us permission to call them whenever panic descends.

We will know we are properly loved when we can wake up at 3.30 a.m. and have the right no longer to be completely alone with our racing hearts and fearsome anxieties.

* * *

We shouldn't be so surprised at the enormous levels of mental illness at large in society; we need only get clear how bad we collectively are at love, how poor we are at lending sympathy, at listening, at offering reassurance, at feeling compassion and at forgiving – and conversely how good we are at hating, shaming and neglecting. We consider ourselves civilised but display levels of love that would shock a primitive tribe or a den of thieves.

Furthermore, we've opted to wash our hands of the issue of love and handed responsibility for healing wholesale to scientists, as though they could culture a complete solution to mental unwellness through their medication. We ignore that the cure largely lies in the emotional realm: in getting better at appeasing each other's fears, at being generous about our transgressions, at no longer tormenting and maltreating one another for our failures and at sitting together through the darkness in a spirit of care and kindly forbearance.

6.
Community

One of the cruellest aspects of mental illness is that it strips us of any ability to believe that other people might be suffering in the way we are. We aren't being wilfully egocentric or arrogant; we are condemned by our illness to a feeling that we are uniquely pitiful, uniquely unacceptable, uniquely awful. The central legacy of mental illness, and a major contributor to our suicidal impulses, is a feeling of exceptionalism.

When we are ill, we avoid other people. Gatherings become impossible, for we grow pre-emptively terrified of the presumed invulnerability and judgementalness of those we might meet. We can't possibly make small talk or concentrate on what someone else is saying when our heads are filled with catastrophic scenarios and an intrusive voice is telling us that we should die. There seems no compact or acceptable way to share with old friends what we have been going through: they knew us as chatty and optimistic. What would they make of the tortured characters we have become? We start to assume that no one on earth could possibly know – let alone accept – what it is like to be us. This is especially tragic because one of the central cures for mental illness is company. Our illness denies us access to precisely what we most need in order to get better.

In 1892, the Swiss artist Ferdinand Hodler exhibited *The Disappointed Souls*. Five figures are pictured in varied states of dejection. We don't know what has gone wrong in their lives, but Hodler invites us to imagine possibilities: a troubled marriage here, a social disgrace there, a depression, a feeling of overwhelming anxiety …

However awful the individual stories might be, the true horror of the painting emerges from the way each crisis is unfolding in complete isolation from its neighbours. The disconsolate figures are only millimetres away from one another, but they might as well be in other countries. It should be so easy to reach out, to share the burden, to lend a comforting hand, to swap stories – and it would be so life-giving. But no fellowship seems possible in this insular hell. Sadness has wrapped each sufferer up in a pitiless sense of their own singularity.

Hodler wasn't painting any one scene; he intended his work as an allegory of modern society as a whole, with its absence of community, its lonely cities and its alienating technologies. But in this very depiction lies the possibility of redemption. We will start to heal when we realise that we are always close to someone who is as wretched as we are. We should hence be able to reach out to a similarly broken neighbour and lament in unison. We should learn to come together for a very particular kind of social occasion whose whole focus

Ferdinand Hodler, *The Disappointed Souls*, 1892

would be an exchange of notes on the misery and lacerations of existence.

In an ideal gathering of the unwell, in a comfortable, safe room, we would take it in turns to reveal to one another the torments in our minds. Each of us would detail the latest challenges. We'd hear of how others were going through sleepless nights, were unable to eat, were too terrified to go outside, were hearing voices and had to fight against constant impulses to kill themselves. The material would be dark, no doubt, but to hear it would be a balm for our stricken, lonely souls.

Ideally, we would keep meeting the same people, week after week, so that our lives would grow entwined with theirs and we could exchange mutual support as we travelled through the valleys of illness. We would know who was in particular difficulty, who needed tenderness and who might benefit from an ordinary-sounding chat about the garden or the weather.

It isn't possible that we are as alone as we currently feel. Biology doesn't produce complete one-offs. There are fellow creatures among the 7 billion of our species. They are there, but we have lost confidence in our right to find them. We feel isolated not because we are so but because we are unwell. We should dare to believe that a fellow disappointed soul is right now sitting next to us on the bench, waiting for us to make a sign.

7.
Psychotherapy

The discipline of psychotherapy has a deserved place at the centre of many accounts of a return to mental health. However, we should clarify what moves are typically made under the umbrella term of 'psychotherapy', and which of these are especially helpful during our moments of desperation.

Honesty

Some of the reason why we may have fallen ill is because of the scale of the lies we have had to tell the world about ourselves – not in order to deceive, but more in order not to shock or offend. Our illness masks a truth that is struggling to break through a compliant exterior. There is so much that we are meant to be but are not. There is so much that we are meant to feel but don't. In the gap between our notion of respectability and our own reality, there grows silence, shame, anxiety and guilt.

In private, we may be terrified of being exposed as incompetent at work while having to maintain an aura of poise in front of colleagues. We may be frustrated with a partner or a parent while under pressure to show only consideration and calm. There may be a secret in our sex lives that seems incompatible with what we hear discussed in the media or among our friends.

Therapy should at last allow us to be honest. We can finally tell someone else the secrets that have pained us for too long. We can tell a non-judgemental, judicious, wise observer about the appalling terrors that we have been going through and the incongruous thoughts that run through our minds. We don't need to be afraid of upsetting or surprising the therapist; they have seen all this before and much more. We can tell them about the crying in the night, the longing to be dead, the anxiety that strikes every morning, the fear of failure, the nature of our sexual tastes. We don't have to be cheerful, competent, restrained or admirable. We can be ourselves, in all our complexity and strangeness. We can regress, complain and lament, without fear of censorship and condemnation. We can start to heal ourselves through honesty.

True and false selves

The psychoanalyst Donald Winnicott made a distinction between what he termed a 'true' and a 'false' self. In order to be healthy, a baby and developing child needs to be allowed to express and experience its true self. That is, it has to be honest about its actual wishes and desires, without fear of censorship or any pressure to compromise. If it is feeling furious, it should have a tantrum. If it is sad, it should weep. If it is envious, it should snarl. It should be allowed the luxury to express its genuine emotions in all their raw intensity. Later on, of course, the child will have to be taught about manners and the feelings of others.

Gradually, but only gradually, it will be shown the way to adopt – at points – a false self that knows how to smile, say thank you and not let on about its disagreements. But only if the true self has had its say for a good long while can development be healthy. Winnicott knew that too many of us are wandering the world without having had the chance to be appropriately awkward and tricky with others before the demand to be polite set in. Going 'mad' for a while may be our attempt to return to some of the feelings that we had to surrender too soon in the name of not angering or upsetting parental figures. Therapy can offer us a second chance to recover contact with the true self and rage and cry as much as we need to.

Questioning our stories

We tend to be imprisoned by a set of stories and judgements that we repeat to ourselves without even noticing how partial and usually unfair they are to us, and how open they might be to being questioned and nuanced. For example, we may tell ourselves that 'Respectable people don't have those sorts of sexual urges,' or 'Good jobs are always unenjoyable,' or 'No really good person would ever want to leave this kind of relationship,' or, more bluntly and definitively, 'You are an ugly failure.'

We may not even know we're carrying such narrow and punitive notions within us, but a good therapist will identify them and gently probe at their logic, opening a sanity-restoring degree of space in our imaginations. They will raise new possibilities with us: Might it not be OK to want something different sexually? Why not contemplate leaving a job that is evidently making us miserable? Must this relationship be forever? Why? Is it really true that we have never done anything with our lives? Might we not be deserving and attractive?

We may never have shown anyone the peculiar arguments that reverberate inside us and make us feel so hemmed in. But speaking these arguments to an outsider can help us to see their absurdity and cruelty, and break their unwarranted spell over us.

The stranglehold of the past

Small children are incomparable learning machines, picking up language, motor and social skills at an exponential rate in their early months and years. They are wholly porous to their environments so that they can learn French and European table manners in Paris and Inuit and fishing techniques in Iqaluit. But this very porousness also makes them perilously vulnerable to the emotional peculiarities of their families. We generalise outwards from dubious premises. One particularly difficult father or mother can shape our expectations of men or women over a lifetime. Being emotionally neglected by a distracted parent can instil a lasting sense of worthlessness, which no amount of later attention or fame can easily contradict. A fear of a volatile parent's temper can mould a whole personality in the direction of meekness and over-compliance.

The therapist's role is to incite the patient to get curious about the strangeness and partiality of their introduction into the world. What they might have believed was 'normal' was in fact the result of a very particular and problematic set of circumstances. We are granted the right to question the sanity of our early caregivers, and in the process, to recover some of our own.

We may have inherited a script from childhood that dictates that we should only ever fall in love with people who leave us emotionally unfulfilled, or that we should start to panic that we will be attacked and humiliated the moment that we do well professionally. Our script may tell us that no one will understand if we level a complaint against them, or that we should betray anyone on whom we have come to depend.

A therapist can open our eyes to the way we may be following a script simply because it feels familiar, not because it is rational or in any way connected up to our satisfaction, and thereby offer us a chance to invent newer and more satisfying ways to lead our lives.

Sorrow for ourselves

We may learn that we are ill because we have been brave for far too long. We have not been allowed fully to appreciate the difficulties we navigated – a depressed parent, a jealous sibling, a bullying classmate – and so have not shown ourselves the compassion and sorrow we should always have been owed. We may need to cry long and hard about the past until the present ceases to seem so universally dark.

Anger at others

Likewise, we may need to feel a fury that has gone cold and congealed inside us. Small children tend never to blame those who have harmed them. They depend on them far too much to dare to question their authority. They turn the hurt in on themselves; they wonder – for example – why they aren't good enough, rather than wondering what business an adult has in humiliating and crushing the spirit of a 4-year-old. The intervention of a therapist can bring an earlier cruelty and illogicality fully to light and therefore permits some of the anger to be redirected from the self – where it might have been the source of self-hatred – back towards its true target. No longer needing to worry about retribution from an overbearing or fragile parent and assured of the justice of our feelings, we can take the risk of being, for a time, as angry as our mental health requires.

A second mind

It may sound odd or impolite to suggest that most of us, when we are in the grip of mental illness, are no longer capable of thinking. That's not how it feels, of course. From the inside, our minds have probably never seemed so busy and so focused. From the moment we wake up in panic and self-disgust, we are ruminating, pondering, exploring catastrophic scenarios, scanning our past, attacking ourselves for things we have done and not done, questioning our legitimacy, talking to ourselves about how repulsive we are, paying attention to voices, inner and outer, recommending that we are evil and sick and headed for the worst, and wondering how and whether we should kill ourselves. Our minds don't give us a moment of respite. We may rub our temples to cool them down and, when eventually we fall asleep at night, we are exhausted by the marathons our thoughts have run inside us.

Nevertheless, we may still want to insist (for the kindest and most redemptive of reasons) that we have not been thinking at all, that none of this hive of activity deserves the title of thinking; it is just illness.

To be mentally ill is to be swamped by secretions of fear, self-hatred and despair that knock out all our higher faculties, all our normal ability to sensibly distinguish one thing from another, to find perspective, to weigh arguments judiciously, to see the wood for the trees, to correctly assess danger, to plan realistically for the future, to determine risks and opportunities and, most importantly, to be kind and generous to ourselves.

None of these faculties function any longer, but – and this is the true nastiness of the illness – we are not always clearly alerted to our loss. We are both very ill and very unaware. It looks as though we are continuing to think as we have always done – with all the usual intelligence and reliability – but that we just have a lot more to worry about. Nowhere along the way does our mind do us the honour of telling us that it has begun to look at reality through a distorted lens, that it has – at some point in the day – to all effects stopped working. No bell goes off; no hazard lights start to flash.

Yet the truth is that we have lost command of a significant part of our minds and are pulling together our ideas from the most degenerate, traumatised, unreliable and vicious aspects of ourselves. It's as if a group of terrorists had donned white coats and were impersonating prestigious scientists in order to lay out a set of vicious theories and prognoses.

Once we have been through a few cycles of distorted thinking and recovered contact with reality, we should do ourselves the kindness of accepting that – on an intermittent basis – we will lose command of our higher faculties and that there is nothing embarrassing in recognising the possibility and accommodating ourselves to it.

We should start to get better at detecting when illness might be drawing in, what the triggers for it might be. Then, when it is upon us, we should do and decide nothing. We shouldn't start to send emails, deliver judgement on our lives or plan for the future. We should – as much as possible – stop all mental activity and rest. We might listen to music, have a long bath, watch something untaxing on television and perhaps take a calming pill.

We should also try to plug our brain into that of someone else, to benefit from their greater powers of reason. We should have a trusted friend or therapist whom we can call on at such moments and ask them if they might recalibrate and regulate our thoughts with an injection of their wisdom and insight. We should willingly put them in charge of determining how things are for us: they should be allowed to tell us what we are worth, what we have done, what there is to worry about – and that we should do our best to discount the doom-laden signals that come from inside us. They may come up with innovative ideas of which we're no longer capable – and that could save us. They might tell us that it's OK to have secrets or that compromise is not always a disaster – concepts that our panicked minds would have had no way of conceptualising.

We should strive to become thinkers who recognise when they are no longer able to think.

Foreboding vs remembering

One common kind of mental illness (which doesn't present itself as an illness to us, of course; it's far too clever for that) leads us to worry incessantly about the future: to fret about bankruptcy, disgrace, physical collapse and abandonment. What is pernicious about this kind of worrying is that it picks up on genuine features of the here and now; it presents itself as reasonable, but, on closer examination, it clearly isn't.

There are always a few alarming things going on: there is some turbulence in the economy, there can be things that go wrong with bodies, reputations do rise and fall ... But what should eventually alert us to the peculiarity of our position is the duration, scale and repetitiveness of our worries. We should learn to see that we are essentially worried all the time about something. The target may shift, but what is constant is our insecurity about existence.

It is in such situations that a therapist may make a useful intervention: they may point out that the way we worry about the future tells us a huge amount about our past. More specifically, we are worried right now in a way that mirrors the panic we once felt as children; we are greeting the challenges of the adult world with the defenceless panic of the child we once were. What we are doing in the process is exchanging the pain of remembering the difficult past for a sense of foreboding around the future; the catastrophe we fear is going to happen has already happened. So sealed off are our memories, we project them forward, where they greet us as apprehensions of what is to come, rather than identifying themselves as legacies of unmasterable past anxiety.

The good therapist becomes aware of the correct source of the anxiety, and doesn't let go of their insight. They will listen politely and generously to our description of our current panic: What will happen in our job? Have we studied enough? What if our enemies gang up on us? But then they will gently try to shift the conversation to the past, to show us that the future looks so fearful because we are being counterproductively loyal to the terrors of an earlier age, which we now need to remember, to feel sad about and then eventually to mourn and move on from.

We should be disloyal to those who brought us up in an atmosphere of fear in order to save what remains of life from always appearing doom-laden: we may be trying to stay close to them by continuing to panic alongside them, but we owe it to ourselves to break the circle of worry and to make our future different from the past, by remembering, localising and mourning what belonged to yesterday even as it pretended to be about tomorrow.

What benefit is there in your illness?

To ask someone who is severely mentally unwell, 'What benefit is there in your illness?' could sound like the height of nastiness. The suggestion appears to be that perhaps the sufferer is gaining some nefarious advantage from their stated infirmity; not only are they missing out on their lives, they are being accused of benefiting from doing so.

Nevertheless, the question can be raised from the kindest and most sincere motives. Mental illnesses can be at once hugely inconvenient and nevertheless protective of some unhealthy dynamics to which we are attached, through our difficult histories. They can prevent us from gaining access to things that we really want but that once upon a time carried an impossible cost – and may therefore still appear unfairly out of bounds to us today. They can be attempts to ward off the dangers of fulfilment imposed on us by our psychological pasts.

A brilliant scholar might fall prey to an obsessive compulsive disorder days before their final examinations. Or someone who wanted to separate from their spouse might develop a severe depression that made them unable to get out of bed to see a lawyer. Or someone might wreck their career through paranoid fears. These might sound like unfortunate coincidences. But psychotherapists are trained to detect unconscious strategies where others might merely see accidents. Our family scripts may have trained us to take early retirement from goals that could be fulfilling but at the same time threatening to someone we loved or depended upon. A mother might have become intensely jealous of her daughter's academic success, and therefore needed her to fail in order to shore up her own fragile esteem. A father might have been jealous of his son's nascent sexual prowess and needed to ensure that the boy would never be satisfied in an area that he had failed in.

'Health' can threaten to unleash competition or a need for confrontation. The therapist's role is to propose to us that we no longer have to face the stark choices of the past and can dare to enjoy a measure of fulfilment without endangering our lives or anyone else's.

Revisiting our younger selves

For many of us, childhood was a confusing and lonely time; we were placed in circumstances that far outstripped our abilities to understand, contextualise and properly apportion blame. As a result, we may have grown up fundamentally mistaken about who we are and what we might deserve.

Understanding our past can involve learning to go back to the child we once were, seeing ourselves in all our early helplessness and confusion and bringing ourselves the benefit of adult compassion and insight. We can take inspiration from the work of Japanese photographer Chino Otsuka, who, in a project called *Imagine Finding Me*, located old pictures of herself in a variety of childhood settings and then inserted herself next to the child she once was. Thirty-three-year-old Otsuka slipped in beside 10-year-old Otsuka outside a boulangerie in Paris; she popped up next to her on a beach in Japan and, one winter, gave her a hand with a snowman she was building after a heavy snowfall.

In our own way, we could imagine that the older us could once have been there beside the younger us. How extraordinary it would have been if we could have given our comparatively frail and naïve self the benefit of our adult strength, experience, poise and confidence; if only we could have returned to give ourselves some answers, to explain to the adults around us – and, at points, to offer ourselves a consoling hug. We would be in a better position now to navigate the confusions and trials of growing up. We would tell ourselves not to worry; we would guarantee that we were lovable and precious; we would hold ourselves through the long nights.

Chino Otsuka, *1980 and 2009, Nagayama, Japan*, from the series *Imagine Finding Me*, 2009

Chino Otsuka, *1982 and 2005, Paris, France*,

from the series *Imagine Finding Me*, 2005

Chino Otsuka, *1976 and 2005, Kamakura, Japan*, from the series *Imagine Finding Me*, 2005

It seems like such a task could be merely fantastical in nature, but far from it. It has an immediate practical application in therapy. The reality is that our childhood self still exists. Their ghost still wanders around the old holiday destinations; they're still having bath time in the old house; they're still at school on winter mornings and they are still crying at night in bed. No part of us ever really dies; they continue at some concurrent level in the unconscious, and will cause us pain so long as they remain fearful and abandoned.

The priority is therefore to imagine going back and standing beside our younger selves in all their difficulties. We should slip into our bed the night we were sobbing after having been shouted at; we should take ourselves to school and sit at the desk next to ours and tell ourselves what we so needed to hear but never did. We should stand up to particular adults and make the speeches we were too inarticulate to utter. Our lost, sad child is still inside us and won't let us rest until we have been able to witness and appease them.

Through therapy, we will start to get better once we have found the scenes that truly matter – and comforted and reparented ourselves back to health.

* * *

For all these life-saving functions of therapy, we should add that most therapists will not match the exalted hopes we harbour of them. This merely reflects the realities of the distribution of talent, which we should be ready for and accommodate ourselves to. Just as we can have the highest estimation of art, but still find most practising artists mediocre, so most therapists we will come across are likely to be less than what they should be.

We should not despair or blame the profession as a whole; we should trust our instincts, politely leave and keep searching until we find someone who combines kindness, intellectual grit, humour, insight, warmth – and an ability to guide us masterfully back to our younger, traumatised selves. We will be very lucky if we find this therapeutic figure at once, but the eventual prize should make even the longest search worthwhile.

8.
Modernity

People have fallen prey to mental illness for as long as our species has been in existence, so it could sound naïve or punitive to single out any one era as especially responsible for generating mental troubles.

Nevertheless, certain periods of history seem capable of bringing together such a confluence of aggravating factors and of so perfectly testing our emotional limits that they deserve to be considered as causes of mental unwellness in and of themselves.

Such may be the case with our own era, a time known as modernity, which, notwithstanding its extraordinary technological creativity, overall peaceability and increasing wealth, has imperilled our mental health as few ages before it ever have. The illnesses bequeathed to us by modern times may manifest themselves very personally within us, but many of their causes lie in the broader dynamics of society, economics and politics.

We would do well to identify the many ways in which our age renders our mental lives more challenging than they should be, and then find techniques to sidestep the worst of our contemporary ills.

Limitless ambition

The hallmark of modernity has been its impatience with anything that might set limits on human achievement. Whereas past ages resigned themselves to offering modest destinies to most of their citizens, modernity has insisted that everyone – whatever their background or families of origin – should be capable of realising the most stellar feats. No longer should anything – education, background, race, creed – stand in the way of ambition.

This has been in its way an incomparably generous philosophy. But it has also, in the background, set up the ideal preconditions for mental instability. It is one thing to promise us all a chance of success; it is another to hint, as our era subtly does, that a modest destiny is essentially unacceptable. While praising lives of outsized accomplishment, our era has thrown a shadow over the ordinary lives that most of us will by necessity continue to have. The norm has ceased to be enough. We cannot be average without at the same time having to think of ourselves as being what our age resents above all else: losers.

Meritocracy

For most of history, it was accepted that what happened to people in their lives was mostly beyond their control or responsibility. The matter lay in the hands of the gods or of fortune, of luck or (more likely) of rigged odds. No one expected the world to be 'fair', and so it was natural to offer sympathy to oneself and others at the inevitable moments of failure.

Modernity has refused to accept this state of affairs. It has fought with unparalleled energy (in education and business, politics and family life) to create a world that can be deemed just; one in which those who deserve to get to the top are able to rise, and where rewards are rightfully apportioned to the most deserving candidates.

Though this too may sound like an advance, it carries a nasty sting in its tail, for if one is committed to believing in an order of things in which those who achieve success invariably deserve to do so, then one is simultaneously signing onto a vision of existence in which those who fail must – with equal fairness – deserve their fate. In a meritocracy, an element of justice enters into the distribution of punishment as well as rewards.

The burden of personal responsibility grows exponentially and explains why this age has seen a corresponding increase in rates of suicide – for the blame for a life that has gone awry can only reside within each of us. We can no longer look elsewhere to explain why we have floundered; we can no longer blame the gods or bad luck. Winners make their own luck, goes the modern mantra – and so we must logically also pay the full, unmitigated price for our failures.

Envy

For most of history, we were protected from the ravages of envy by a class structure that denied most of life's advantages to all but a narrow and preselected few. Most of us had very little, but we also knew that there was no alternative to penury and that it was therefore not for us to gape with longing and desire at those with finer homes and carriages, horses and titles.

Modernity has freed us from such class-bound strictures. We are repeatedly informed that we are all born equal, and therefore can and should aspire to the most gilded lives and compare ourselves to everyone else in our societies. We no longer believe in innate aristocrats or born peasants; we are runners on a level playing field, able to reach whatever result we aim for depending on our investments of imagination and energy. This means that the eventual gaps in social status and material wealth are no longer, as they used to be in the past, an unremarkable feature of the natural order; they are a devastating reminder that the good life has eluded our grasp.

It becomes painful and at points intolerable to read up about old school acquaintances who may now be scaling the heights while we remain – for causes we cannot overcome – tethered to more lowly stations. We are condemned to perpetual envy and inadequacy in a radically unequal world of self-declared equals.

Cheerfulness

Past ages knew to give a wide space for sadness and melancholy in the experience of every human. Life was understood to be, for the most part, about regret, longing, failure, incompleteness and sadness. Buddhism declared that life itself was suffering; the Judeo-Christian tradition emphasised that we were all the heirs of Adam and Eve, broken and tarred by sin, condemned to grief outside the gates of paradise. The situation was dark but – crucially – communally so. There was no danger of feeling isolated with one's woes; to exist was automatically to sign up to suffering.

Modernity has heroically thrown off such inbuilt pessimism; it is an age of resolute good cheer, of a faith in the future and of our power to overcome whatever challenges we face through willpower and technology. Pessimism has been recategorised as a disease.

But though the trajectory of humankind may – arguably – be on an upward curve, the arc of every life never manages to escape fearsome degrees of pain and loss. The human race may be getting happier, but each one of us remains exposed to a devastating range of sorrows. Except that there is now an added burden in weeping when we are meant to smile and in wanting to hide when others are insisting that we step out and celebrate. Our sadness starts to seem like a personal curse rather than what it more fairly always is: an inevitable feature of being alive.

Secularism

To further aggravate our emotional woes, modernity – particularly in Western culture – has thrown aside what was, since the dawn of time, a central resource for coping with life's vicissitudes. For many, God no longer exists, and there is now little we can turn to, intone in front of or beg for deliverance from when times grow hard. We dwell in a world ruled by the pitiless laws of science, where relief is only on offer from psychotherapists or psychiatrists, who equate our problems narrowly with our own personal histories and biology. It feels (for most of us) impossible to weep in temples and churches. We scour the universe for clues as to why we are here and what we are meant to do with our troubles and hear back only static and silence.

At the same time, the disappearance of religion means that humankind looms ever larger in our own imaginations. There is nothing left to relativise us. We used to be put in our places by contact with the spiritual realm. Every weekend, we would be shepherded into gloriously rendered halls and reminded of what a puny thing humanity was, how ridiculous were all our achievements and how flawed and frail we were next to the majesty of God. The differences between human beings were as nothing next to the differences between us and the almighty; we were usefully relativised by the shadow of the divine.

Now humankind is the measure of all things. Our heroes are only drawn from our own kind, our myths reference only ourselves and our strengths. We receive few lessons in perspective and modesty, and lose our sanity in the gap between what we are meant to be and what almost all of us end up remaining.

Loneliness

In the past, we could not survive without the group. Our natural frailty meant that we would need to lean on the family and community in order to survive. It made for oppression at points, but it also spared us modernity's recurrent risks of alienation and isolation.

We have grown ever more capable of subsisting without others; we can endure for days in cities of 10 million people without uttering a word. Yet we have lost the art of admitting our sorrows to others and of building connections based on vulnerability. We are lucky if we can lay claim to even one or two people we can call on when disaster strikes.

Our age attempts to cure loneliness through romantic love, the promise that we may find one very special person to whom we can tie ourselves for life and who will spare us the need for anyone else. But this emphasis only serves to aggravate our isolation and renders our relationships more fractious than they should be, for no single person, however extraordinary, can ever replace our need for a broader circle of support. We fail to bring the most important parts of ourselves to our friendships; we starve ourselves of the solace and salvation of the many in a misguided search for the one.

The chatter

So seriously does our age take itself, it doesn't cease talking of its own melodramas and triumphs with a mesmerising and maddening intensity. We have surrounded ourselves with gadgets that give us minute-by-minute insights into the perturbed and excited minds of billions of others, and that along the way deny us all necessary access to stillness, distance and perspective, let alone time for self-knowledge and reflection.

We grow convinced of the importance of everything in the near term and can set nothing in its broader context. We pass our own mental perturbations on to one another under the guise of keeping one another 'informed'. The media spreads our madness virally and without respite. We come under pressure to know at all times 'what is going on', without realising how much we have abandoned ourselves to an enervating collective frenzy at the cost of our serenity and self-possession.

So pernicious are the trends of modernity, so much do they affect our chances of mental well-being, that sanity demands that we exercise immense caution around our era and – as quietly as we need to – enter a state of what could be termed internal exile from some of its pressures. We may continue to benefit from the advantages of the modern age while carving out a wide berth between ourselves and its more destructive psychological ideals.

As part of such distancing manoeuvres, we might stick to some of the following counter-cyclical ideas:

Modesty

We know the attractions of extraordinary lives well enough: the glamour, the acclaim, the material abundance … What can be less familiar to us are their costs: the destruction of emotional stability, the frenetic activity, the lack of time in which to absorb our experiences, the envy and hostility that success arouses, the fear of retribution and the dread of downfall.

Once we have properly surveyed the merits and demerits on offer, we may choose to side with what the modern age typically considers to be a disaster – a quiet life – not from a lack of ambition, but from a more focused aspiration for what we recognise to be the primary ingredient of happiness: peace of mind.

We might choose to live outside a large metropolis, not to push ourselves forward for promotion, avoid the limelight and do a satisfactory but undramatic kind of work. We can discover the subtle greatness of a life in which we exercise our virtues on a domestic canvas, in which we do not seek to be known by people we don't ourselves know and in which the intricate love of a few carefully chosen souls replaces the hurried attentions of a host of unfaithful strangers. In such quiet lives, we can go to bed early, we don't need to attend functions with people we despise, we work only for the money we need to secure a materially adequate standard of living, we drop out of the status race and refuse to assess ourselves according to the alien standards of a corrupting media.

We will have liberated ourselves from the madness of the age when we can look on loud and heroic lives – perhaps led by people we once knew – and with good faith say that this is not for us, that we are happier where we are, because we understand what we require to survive mentally: cosiness, connection and an ongoing lack of drama.

Self-acceptance

We know well enough the modern mantra that we are what we earn and that we count only in relation to the scale of our achievements. But it is open to us also to question this so-called meritocratic logic and to look to a more generous point of view, wherein we may be able to count simply on the basis that we exist – and that our destiny, be it stellar or damned, should not be the measure of the whole of us.

We can throw off the idea that we always get what we deserve, and that any reversal has to be judged as earned and therefore labelled just. We can accept the truth of an extraordinary redemptive idea that the modern age cannot tolerate: that it might be possible to fail in the eyes of the world and yet to remain valuable and deserving of love.

Community

Every time we share a piece of our pained inner self with a like-minded friend, we defend ourselves against despair and self-hatred. It should matter to us far less whether we have found one special romantic partner; what we need is a network of non-judgemental souls who have known enough of their own suffering to be ready to show us compassion and tenderness when we stumble.

Perspective

We need to puncture the self-importance of the age with regular contact with older, deeper, wider sources of feeling: through contact with a natural world that pursues its own priorities with little reference to our own sagas, through the reading of history books that shrink our modern-day adventures and convulsions to a more manageable and rightful size – and through travel to countries that take no interest in our own peculiar national preoccupations, scandals and triumphs.

An internal hut

In order properly to escape modernity, we might seek to move to a hut somewhere far away. We would be in nature, with our own thoughts and – ideally – a circle of supportive friends. We would not need to be harried and pressured to conform to foreign ideals of success. But moving ourselves physically may not be necessary. What we may need is not so much an actual hut as a hut inside our own minds, to which we can retreat when we know that we are being assailed by values that are inimical to our balance and self-love. We may continue to wander through the modern world, to all intents and purposes just another obedient citizen of its value system, while internally highly suspicious of the messages we are receiving and committed to replacing them with ones imbued with far greater kindness and justice.

We can blame ourselves too much for our mental suffering. We are not merely personally fragile. We are living through a high-tech age that routinely smashes its more sensitive members to pieces through adherence to what will one day be recognised as a grossly primitive and unimaginative value system.

9.
Self-Compassion

If there is one generalisation we can hazard of those who end up mentally unwell, we could say that they are masters at being very nasty to themselves.

The worst kind of nastiness doesn't have to involve shouting at oneself or calling oneself an idiot, though this might happen too. It means that one part of us continually drives the other towards self-doubt, fear, paranoia, shame and despair, without revealing that it is doing this or that there might be other options available. Panic and self-flagellation become identified with safety and virtue. No attention is drawn towards the partiality of the choices that are being made internally, or the game would be up. Self-loathing may be the order of the day, but it is never presented as such; we just think we are 'normal', hard-headed and interpreting reality as it truly is.

Release from the grip of self-loathing therefore has to start with a growing awareness of what we are doing to ourselves, and what the alternatives might be. For example, we might start to notice that no sooner has something nice happened to us than we set about wondering when something awful will strike in revenge; that every success has to be ruined by a feeling of foreboding and guilt; that every potentially pleasant day ends up marred by panic or a sense of loss; that we spontaneously imagine that everyone must hate us and that the worst things are being said about us the moment we leave any room.

On the surface, none of this looks like 'nastiness'. We could just say that we have a 'worried mind', or a 'regretful temperament'. But it is useful to group these ideas under a singular title in order fully to identify the direction in which they point: towards the systematic destruction of any pleasure in being ourselves, which is a very nasty thing to do to someone. Without realising it, we are committed to throttling all our chances of contentment at the earliest opportunity. We dwell inside a mind in which every good element has to be spoilt and every vicious, destructive, alarming and cruel thought has to be honoured.

As an experiment, we might imagine trying to be as kind as possible towards our own minds, to see how differently things might unfold. Rather than dragging every last deformed and mean idea into the theatre of consciousness, we could only present our minds with the very kindest and most reassuring ideas. The moment we left a room, we might be ruthless in preventing thoughts about our unacceptability from manifesting themselves in the usual way; they might be begging to be let in (and claiming all sorts of reasons why they should be so), but, for once, we could give them a firm 'no'. If they kept trying to make their way into our minds, we might put on a piece of music or do some gardening – anything other than allow destructive concepts to have their normal rule over us.

Likewise, when the old familiar thought about the future being terrible knocked at the door, we'd refuse to let it in; when we woke up with the traditional burden of guilt about our past mistakes, we'd not pay attention. We'd realise that we had agency over the things that fill our minds and that we don't have to surrender control to our masochistic stage manager at every turn.

Along the way, we might start to appreciate that other people do not give their worst thoughts unlimited sway. They don't give endless time to ideas of their own dreadfulness and their likely destruction. They don't allow whole days to be lost in catastrophic forebodings. One way to capture the reason for this is that they are, fundamentally, *kind to themselves*; they are not in the business of torturing their own spirits.

Where does this unconscious impulse to be unkind to ourselves come from? How is the choice to torture ourselves made? We can hazard another generalisation. The way we treat ourselves is an internalisation of the way others once treated us, either directly in the sense of how they spoke to us, or indirectly, in the sense of how they behaved around us, which could have included ignoring us or openly displaying a preference for someone else.

Our early caregivers did not literally instruct us in having to worry about our right to exist or tell us to panic constantly about what might happen next. But the way that our minds now work bears the imprint of their relationship to us; it is an extrapolation from their messages of fear and ridicule, humiliation and shame, of which we have been such careful students.

To get a measure of where we stand on the spectrum of self-love, we need only ask ourselves a very simple question (that we have nevertheless ignored for far too long): How much do I like myself? If the answer immediately and intuitively comes back that we feel loathsome, there is a history that we urgently need to consider and are choosing to ignore. The contempt we habitually show ourselves is neither fair nor right; we should spot the oddity and partiality of treating ourselves with a viciousness we wouldn't accord to our worst enemies.

This self-hatred breeds low self-confidence and a continual fear of disaster. Terrible things, after all, must happen to terrible people. We are denied any confidence in ourselves as workers, parents, friends and humans more broadly, and are terrified both whenever things go well (because our comeuppance is sure to be just around the corner) and when we contemplate the future (which must be filled with dreadful and threatening prospects). It is one of the more unexpected features of mental life that what manifests itself as anxiety, in many cases, is really just an expression of intense self-suspicion.

For a long time, self-hatred can be hidden within an outwardly normal life. The destruction blends in. But just how dangerous and unfair we are being to ourselves is likely to come to the fore when we hit a crisis; when we make some sort of mistake or encounter a reversal. At moments when anyone might experience a dip in their degrees of self-love and confidence, we enter a completely different and more perilous zone. The bad news confirms every one of our savage impulses and self-suspicions. It kick-starts efforts conclusively to tear ourselves apart. Not only are we somewhat in trouble and responsible, we are – as we tell ourselves – a catastrophe and despicable, foul and damned. Self-torture can quickly end up with compulsive thoughts of self-extinction.

People who die of suicide are not usually those for whom a few things have gone very wrong; they may have encountered some otherwise survivable reversals, but against a background of fierce self-hatred these events become unendurable. In many cases, it is self-hatred that will end up killing them, not the apparent subjects of their panic and sorrow.

As ever, salvation comes through self-awareness. There is nothing inevitable about self-hatred. We are treating ourselves unkindly because people were in the past not especially kind to us, and we are being touchingly yet dangerously loyal to their philosophies of derision. Harshness can have a glamour all of its own; it can seem the more serious and powerful approach to take towards our characters, as though we were doing ourselves a favour (and even securing our safety) by whipping our consciences as hard as possible.

But if we're to stay alive, we need radically to redraw our moral code and return to kindness the prestige that it should always have had. Kindness to ourselves is the single most necessary quality for success and endurance. That we spent so long on the side of cruelty is a sign not of its utility, but of the scale of the distortions we have inherited from the past. We have learnt far too much about a lack of mercy, about panic, about self-suspicion and finding oneself pitiful. Now – when we have felt the temptations of suicide – we need to rediscover the virtues of forgiveness, mercy, calm and gentleness. And when we panic and feel intensely anxious about the future, we need to remember that we are in essence worrying about our fundamental legitimacy and lovability. Our survival depends on a swift mastery of the art of self-compassion.

10.
Gratitude

A particularly unfortunate consequence of mental illness is its power to close us off from the world, from its beauty, its interest and its power to distract us from ourselves. We are liable to be so engulfed in what feels like a life-or-death struggle, we forget that there is anything outside the walls of our own minds. Every morning is likely to begin with fear and trepidation; it feels like a close-run thing whether we will make it to evening. In the circumstances, there is little chance to observe the dawn, we don't hear the birdsong, we miss that the rising sun briefly dressed up the horizon in a mantle of purple-gold.

Once upon a time, when we were children, we were champions at observation. A simple walk to the park offered a treasury of discoveries. There was the brick wall along which we liked to run our hands; there was an ant that we saw on the pavement and followed until it disappeared into a mysterious hole just wide enough to take its own body; there was a small yellow flower growing in some rubble whose stem we caressed and whose petals we rubbed against our cheek. There were the clouds we observed, stretching and distending themselves like swirls of milk in coffee; there were the three gigantic trees whose weathered bark we ran our nails across and wanted, if we'd been able, to knead and wrap ourselves in.

It can feel as if there is no more time for such frivolities now. Adult life has grown drained of delight. We spend hours poring over emotions with therapists; we visit psychiatric doctors; we sit in ugly rooms discussing our pains with strangers.

It isn't that we have resolutely turned our minds against appreciation. We simply lack encouragement – and, we might say, permission. We need to have it confirmed to us by some external source that it is not trivial to look up from ourselves for a while, that the capacity to find delight in so-called 'small things' is at the core of recovery and strength. Appreciation may once have been automatic, but that isn't an argument against a little artificiality in restarting its engines. We may need to be nudged occasionally to pause with our travails and take a moment to look around. The huge things won't be solved very quickly. We're going to be with anxiety and despair for a little while longer yet, but that is no reason to shun moments of relief.

It is artists who may best stimulate our appetites through evidence of their own heightened sensitivities. We might consider the work of Gustave Caillebotte (1848–1894), an exceptionally generous observer of our place on the earth. He looked closely at summer fruit, skies, the view from the window in midafternoon, the atmosphere in the park. In 1875, while staying in his family's home in Yerres, south of Paris, he went down to the river on a grey day and grew fascinated

Gustave Caillebotte, *The Yerres, Effect of Rain*, 1875

by the patterns made by large drops of summer rain on the surface of the water. We have seen such a sight hundreds of times before, but are unlikely – for a long while at least – to have given it its due, to have been appropriately mesmerised by complex geometries of interlocking circles, by the refractions of light, by the variegated sounds of water falling into water.

Caillebotte's painting isn't about our distress. It knows nothing about the broken relationship with our spouse, our troubles with lawyers, our financial anxieties, our fear of the future. It seems to grasp that such things might exist and yet it insists that they do not – right now – need to swallow the whole of our lives. For a moment or two, we can slip out of ourselves; we can pause on our walk by the riverbank and can take in something that will remind us that it is worth keeping on with existence.

Following Caillebotte's lead, we might sometimes interrupt our internal dialogue in order to study daisies in jars, someone's hands, an old map, a photo from childhood, a pencil on a new sheet of paper. We have suffered so much, we are so aware of all that is difficult and arduous, but we have not been barred from adopting the wide-eyedness of children and artists. Indeed, it is against the backdrop of our difficulties that beauty becomes not just pleasing but moving – a reminder of our true home, to which we so long to return.

In our efforts to appreciate what is still good, we might also take a lead from the exceptionally busy Yinzhen, fifth Emperor of China's Qing dynasty (1678–1735), who was preoccupied with reforming his country's taxation system and rooting out corruption in local officials – but nevertheless found the time to take his son and a few of his favourite courtiers out for a picnic in the fields near Beijing, in order to look at the flowers, at some point around 1725.

It is touching to note the solemn expression of the Emperor, who has interrupted the affairs of state for something as easy to overlook as some spring flowers. Yinzhen was known to have been a deeply pious and serious man, but he evidently retained a secure hold on life's real priorities, nudging us to recalibrate our own hierarchy of importance in the direction of the overlooked beauty of the everyday. If an Emperor can do this, then we, for all our afflictions, can follow too.

Much remains imperfect; most of our lives are not as we would want them to be. But this should not become a reason to refuse modest pleasures; we should be sure to carve out moments when, despite everything, we can still savour incidental arguments for hope, sweetness and an end to suffering.

Anonymous, *The Yongzheng Emperor Admiring Flowers*, c. 1725

11.
Perspective

Those of us who are mentally unwell tend to come under great pressure, from relatives and friends, not to exaggerate our illnesses; the recommendation can boil down to a plea – more or less directly delivered – not to 'make such a big deal of it'.

Yet it is unfortunate that the call to minimise one's illness generally comes from such partial and unsympathetic sources, because, when it is handled with love and with an eye to genuine improvement, the idea of adopting a new perspective on one's troubles can be central to the process of recovery.

Mental illness requires so much of our attention and mobilises so many of our thoughts, it's unsurprising if it also scrambles our sense of priorities and hierarchy for a time. In our most acute phases, we have no option other than to place ourselves at the centre of our drama and to ensure that every other call on us is minimised.

Nevertheless, when the intensity has passed, there are opportunities to step back and consider what has happened from a broader and therefore more consoling perspective. We might keep some of the following contextualising concepts in mind:

Everything human is messed up

At our worst moments, not only do we castigate ourselves for having ruined our lives and made so many mistakes, we compound our misery with an overwhelming certainty: that we are alone in our foolishness. All around us, we think we see only success stories: people we were at school with who are not curled up in bed in a psychiatric ward, people in the newspapers who are handling weighty matters of state with maturity. Our minds might be telling us we're not only mad, but we're also completely alone in the extent of our stupidity.

We need to help ourselves with new perspectives, largely through the help of those overlooked tools for mental healing: history books. Beneath a veneer of competence and purposiveness, almost all human affairs have always been riddled with stupidity, waste, bluster, ego, folly and nastiness. In the small canvas of our own lives, we're experiencing themes that have existed in history as a whole since the start.

To weaken our painful exceptionalism, we might pick up some books about the history of Ancient Rome. There are the impressive aspects, of course: the rapid build-up of foreign colonies, the engineering marvels, the sophisticated villas and literary works. But that cannot for long cover up the blinding stupidity of most of the political class, the mendacity, egoism, short-termism, vanity, lack of imagination and eccentricity, which led with time to the smashing of the temples and the collapse of a civilisation.

The human animal is an endemically flawed creature, and after one has spent weeks focused on one's own shortcomings, it makes sense to open the lens a bit wider and see how every society, enterprise and individual that sets out with ambition and a good heart will, soon enough, come into contact with certain incontrovertible facts about our nature. Our flaws may seem to isolate us, but they actually connect us up directly to all the so-called great figures and ages of history.

There are echoes of our behaviour in pretty much every historical period we might study: in the collapse of the Ming Dynasty, the rise and dissolution of the Kingdom of Benin, the dying days of the Aztecs, the dismemberment of the Navajos, the debacle of the Third French Republic ... Any time a group of people get together and decide to improve the world or build something fine and lasting, we can be sure that disaster and character deficiencies will soon predominate.

We have suffered completely on our own for long enough. We may not be acting rationally, but that's only because we are members of a species that has collectively been doing very destructive and nonsensical things since records began. We might spend an hour a day reading the histories of empires, societies and individuals that can make our dramas less significant – and less dreadful – in our own minds.

Nothing matters

From close up, our failure matters immensely, of course. We're very aware of how badly we disrupted the holidays last week and how many of our friends now know about our condition – and how long it might be till we are back at work. But in order to respect our peace of mind, we will need to disrespect our sense of what is truly, existentially important.

In a 13.7-billion-year-old universe that measures 93 billion light years across and might contain 100 billion galaxies, each containing around 100 billion stars, we and our illness are a mercifully small deal.

Of course, our reversals hurt immensely, but we should drown out any sense of shame in an appreciation of how little truly counts within the vastness of time and space. We can lose some of our painful individuality in contact with what is larger, older, deeper and more mysterious than we are. As part of our recovery, we should look at images of the North Pole from the air, of the Earth from Mars or of a neighbouring galaxy from the Hubble telescope.

In Japan's Shinto religion, it is recommended that the pains of the individual ego should be assuaged through regular contact with the mighty phenomena of nature, which return a reduced self-image to us. In one of Katsushika Hokusai's famous depictions of Mount Fuji (see overleaf), a group of travellers have stopped by a giant cedar tree and – as their religion commands them – are hugging it. They embrace the trunk, losing themselves in its vastness, honouring its strengths and height. They know – and it brings them joy to realise this – that they are puny next to such a mighty natural phenomenon. It will still be around when their great-great-grandchildren are old; it will survive storms and earthquakes, remaining imperturbable on its promontory overlooking Japan's great volcano.

The encounter with the tree will have delayed the travellers. Perhaps the post they are carrying will be a few hours late; maybe they will have to postpone a meeting. But something far more important has come in to replace an immaculate human schedule: a connection with the larger and more mysterious forces of the universe to which we generally pay so little attention, but to which we remain subject and should strive to lose ourselves in so as to alleviate the pressures of our own ambitions and perfectionism.

Puzzles beyond our own

Our illness necessarily absorbs us in the puzzles of our own psyches. We have to spend a lot of time – probably with therapists – attempting to work out forgotten parts of our

Katsushika Hokusai, *Mishima Pass in Kai Province (Kōshū Mishima goe)*, from the series *Thirty-six Views of Mount Fuji*, c. 1830–1832

past and how much it continues to have an impact on the present. We are probably more confused by ourselves than we have ever been; we sense how unpredictable, complicated and multilayered our brains are.

It's because our curiosity is so tied down with working on ourselves that we should take care every now and then to give it new and different targets to exercise itself on. Traditionally, it hasn't come very naturally to humans to get properly curious about what lies outside of us, but we can sense how healthy and life-enhancing it is whenever we can manage to exercise our imaginations on foreign matter.

We might be inspired by the 16th-century French naturalist Pierre Belon, one of the first people to push aside most thoughts in his mind in order to devote himself exclusively to working out the structure and life cycles of fish. In his *On the Nature and Diversity of Fish* (see overleaf), published in Paris in 1555, Belon investigated hundreds of different species that he had hauled from the oceans, dissected and drawn in a charmingly naïve style, speculating on how they fitted into the order of nature.

What is touching is how much Belon got wrong. His book is filled with fish that aren't accurately drawn and conclusions that make no sense to modern science. But this only serves to make Belon more like all of us. He didn't have the full facts at

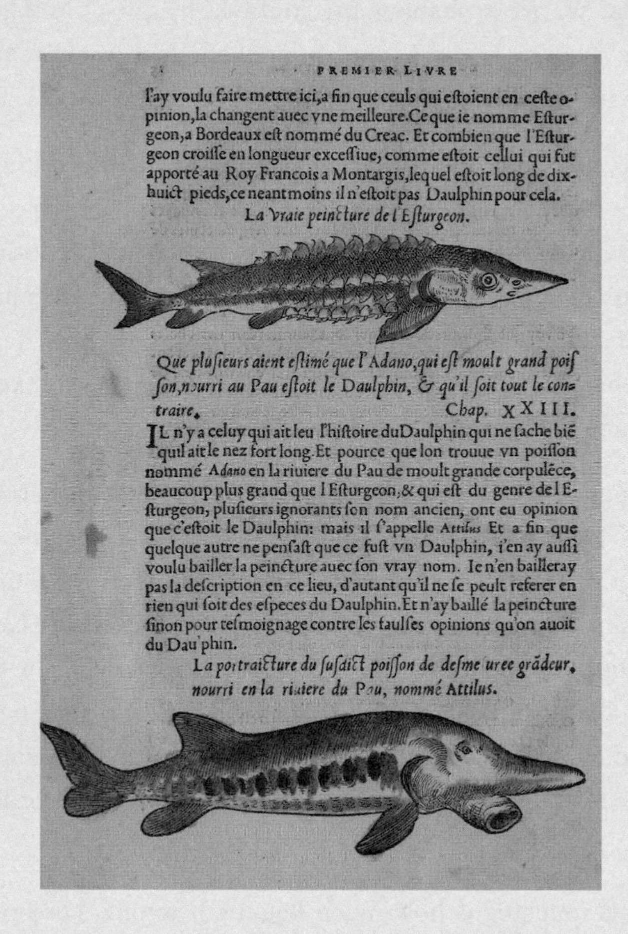

PREMIER LIVRE

I'ay voulu faire mettre ici, a fin que ceuls qui estoient en ceste opinion, la changent auec vne meilleure. Ce que ie nomme Esturgeon, a Bordeaux est nommé du Creac. Et combien que l'Esturgeon croisse en longueur excessiue, comme estoit cellui qui fut apporté au Roy Francois a Montargis, lequel estoit long de dixhuict pieds, ce neantmoins il n'estoit pas Daulphin pour cela.

La Vraie peincture de l'Esturgeon.

Que plusieurs aient estimé que l'Adano, qui est moult grand poisson, nourri au Pau estoit le Daulphin, & qu'il soit tout le contraire. Chap. XXIII.

IL n'y a celuy qui ait leu l'histoire du Daulphin qui ne sache biẽ qu'il ait le nez fort long. Et pource que lon trouue vn poisson nommé *Adano* en la riuiere du Pau de moult grande corpulẽce, beaucoup plus grand que l'Esturgeon, & qui est du genre de l'Esturgeon, plusieurs ignorants son nom ancien, ont eu opinion que c'estoit le Daulphin: mais il s'appelle *Attilus* Et a fin que quelque autre ne pensast que ce fust vn Daulphin, i'en ay aussi voulu bailler la peincture auec son vray nom. Ie n'en bailleray pas la description en ce lieu, d'autant qu'il ne se peult referer en rien qui soit des especes du Daulphin. Et n'ay baillé la peincture sinon pour tesmoignage contre les faulses opinions qu'on auoit du Dauphin.

La portraicture du susdict poisson de desmesuree grãdeur, nourri en la riuiere du Pau, nommé Attilus.

Pierre Belon, a page from *Histoire de la Nature des Estranges Poissons Marins*, 1551 his disposal, yet he didn't let ignorance become an argument against wanting to know more.

A lot more is known now – about fish and everything else – than in Belon's day. However, our task as recovering patients isn't necessarily to become world-class experts in any field; it is to pursue an amateurish interest in some area of knowledge intricate and fascinating enough to absorb us over many hours. It could be fish, but it might be coins, flowers, electronics, Chinese poetry, model railways, calligraphy, Cambodian cooking – anything with the power to tie down our restless minds in puzzles filled with wonder.

We will be called upon to return to our own challenges soon enough, but we will have been refreshed and lightened by an encounter with a mysterious otherness beyond us that, quite as much as knowledge of our deep self, is what we require to achieve inner balance.

12.
Work

Even without knowing the specifics, we can hazard that, somewhere along the line, work will have heavily contributed to our mental illness. At the same time, we can suggest that work, if correctly rethought and reconfigured, may play a central role in our recovery. We should learn to handle this double-edged sword with particular care.

Working to impress

Our emotional difficulties with work tend to begin with the way that it offers us unparalleled chances to impress those who do not, or did not, originally believe in us. It is the favoured tool of all those who start in life with a feeling of being under-loved, under-appreciated and overlooked. It is the instrument of vengeance of the once ignored. Under the guise of a merely practical pursuit, it carries a heavy emotional mission; it is the means by which we try to earn our right to be.

For a while, it may seem to fulfil this purpose very well. Success can earn us preferment, higher income, honour and fame, which can assuage our underlying sense that we are undeserving and shameful.

But the healing is only ever cosmetic and temporary and subject to constant reversals. All success necessarily brings with it envy and criticism. The moment we have achieved a prominent position, dissenting voices will emerge to claim that we are illegitimate and unworthy, and thereby remind us of the negative self-image we are pedalling so hard to outwit. We'll be torn between listening to praise and focusing on the thread of denunciation – and the latter will be the only one that mesmerises us.

No amount of success will be able to expunge our inner sense of baseness and unlovability. We may work monstrously hard not because our material needs are so elevated, but because we only ever feel a few steps ahead of a chorus of inner voices telling us that we are futile and ludicrous.

Over time, we will fall prey to exhaustion. The source of our tiredness won't be the work itself; it will be the constant effort to keep at bay a confrontation with our original lack of self-love. It will simply be too tiring to spend a whole life insisting through our labours that we are not bad people.

Impostor syndrome

Related to such symptoms will be a continuous feeling while at work that we are about to be unmasked as not up to the job that we are claiming to know how to carry out. Whatever our technical competence or years of experience, our emotional state will imbue us with a conviction that we do not deserve the respect and trust of those who depend on us. The gap between what we are claiming to be and what we suspect we are deep down will lead to an increasing sense of anxiety and dread. We may fear being suddenly and publicly unmasked, being denounced anonymously or humiliated whenever our colleagues and enemies choose. Paranoid thoughts will haunt us; we may break out in alarm or be unable to speak in public. In the end, it can feel easier to fail in order to prove our inner voices right rather than continue to defy our latent self-suspicion.

The breakdown

If we are extremely lucky, a breakdown does not need to be merely the end. We will be failing in certain eyes, of course; we'll be letting a lot of people down and violating the hopes of those who need us to perform in a certain way.

But if accompanied by the right sorts of care, a breakdown can allow us to review the role that work was playing in our lives and to cease to use it as a compensation for an emotional wound. We can see that the real tragedy isn't that we messed up our impressive careers, but that we so badly needed to have them in the first place in order to make up for early and unexplored deprivation.

Our failure may have stripped us of chances to impress in the worldly sense. At a stroke, we'll be liberated from those false friends and colleagues who pegged their attentions to our money and status. All that we will have to fall back on are those who understand love and are willing to be concerned with us not because of anything we can do for them, but just because we are alive. This may be the first time this unconditionality has ever been witnessed, and it will correct a lingering misapprehension that we can only earn care through performance.

The breakdown will offer us a path towards a more authentic way of living, where who we really are, shorn of our trappings, can feel acceptable. The failure we always dreaded would happen has unfolded and we are liberated no longer to have to worry about it as a feared spectre.

In the ruins, we may be able to ask ourselves a new question: What do I actually want to do? Whose opinion do I really care about? We will have slain the dragon of prestige; we may be ready to live on our own terms for the first time.

Authentic work

We may have to go back as far as childhood and ask: What did I really enjoy doing? When did I feel most alive? There may be clues as to what our future should be in the way we used to play as small children, when impressing other people and earning money were far from our minds.

We should allow ourselves to think in original ways, casting aside any prejudice as to what a respectable or reasonable job might be. We should be unbothered by fears of failing, for this is a seam we have now fully explored. We should go back to what work should always have been for us – a source of intrinsic satisfaction – before it got saddled with the task of assuring us of our value as a human being in the eyes of an imagined hostile and sceptical audience.

Helping

Our mental troubles will have opened up fresh territories of pain for us. We'll be aware from first-hand experience that a whole subsection of the population is labouring under mental torment, and we may be newly motivated to help them as others have helped us.

We may be able to use our own history of pain to alleviate strangers in their agony, lending our time, empathy, love and curiosity.

We may have doubted that we could ever be of true use to anyone; we partly fell ill because of a basic sense of superfluity. But by targeting work where helping others in grave distress is the priority, we can derive a visceral sense of the difference we can make to someone else's world. We may not be earning as much and people at large may not care a jot, but we'll have all the affirmation we need for ourselves in the knowledge that we are – on a good day – able to lend someone else a reason to live.

Small improvements

Much work seeks to have an impact on a large scale over an extended time period, involving hundreds and perhaps millions of players.

Given our fragility, we might be counselled away from vast and complex efforts. We need tasks that can leave us feeling as if we have made a small but notable difference in someone else's life at the end of every day. Perhaps we have in a modest way improved their command of a language or cleaned up their garden or given them something nourishing to eat. We may not have pushed the boundaries of knowledge or be remembered in a thousand years, but we'll have done something more substantial still: kept ourselves steady against enormous odds and made an honest contribution to the welfare of a few fellow ailing humans.

13.
Pessimism

It may be hard to imagine that the word 'pessimism' could have any role in mitigating the effects of mental illness. But that would be to underestimate the covert persecutory aspects of its opposite, optimism. The expectation that our lives *should* be well, that we *should* be forever free of anxiety and despair, paranoia and loneliness is both understandable in its ambition and confidence – and quietly tormenting.

Those of us who have been visited by severe mental illness need to cling to darker counsel. We, members of a not insubstantial minority, have been stricken by a fragility that will not lightly leave us alone again, and so need to be ready always to greet life with care: grateful for whichever days go well, serene in the face of those that don't, appreciative of the small gains we are capable of and permanently vigilant as to the possibility of relapse. We have been denied the easy-going lives we would have loved to lead and should not add insult to injury by continuing to regret them; they should be mourned rather than lamented.

We should accept with grace that things are not as we would wish them to be. We will have to hobble when we would have loved to gambol freely. We'll need to be creative about exploring how life could be bearable in circumstances far less rosy than anyone would have wished. We will have to give up our pride – that is, our assurance in our own competence and automatic right to dignity. We have been humbled and ridiculed by our own minds.

At the same time, we should take steps to make ourselves at home in the darkness. In a safe environment, perhaps with a therapist, we should willingly expose our reason to our worst, nastiest and most invalid thoughts, rather than let them steal up to us at a time of their choosing. We should practise thought exercises that strip our fears of their unexamined hold on us.

The anxious should accept that they can never eradicate certain risks but that these can be shouldered – and a habitable life made among the ruins. Our relationships may never go right, certain family members will always resent us, particular enemies will never come over to our side, we cannot correct mistakes in our career, there will invariably be doubters and outright sadists. None of this should surprise us; we should not let undue innocence aggravate our mood. We should explore the unbudgeable sadness on sunny mornings when our reasoning faculties are lively and calming, instead of letting matters unnerve us in 3 a.m. confrontations when we are too groggy and worn down to know what to answer our demons.

We should take heed from the knowledge that it has already been very bad and if it were to be so again, we would cope as we have already done. We should take comfort from the thought that we have suffered what some would consider to be the worst scenario – we have actually gone 'mad' – and yet we are still here, more or less coherent, still able to enjoy one or two things, still capable of gratitude and occasional appreciation. Simply on the basis of what we have survived, we should not be very scared of anything much again.

We must accept with grim cheer that it wasn't to be our fate to belong to the mentally robust cohort. When the angels were distributing brains, we were accorded one of the more sensitive, erratic, brilliant, tumultuous ones, which we will have to continue to watch like anxious nurses for the first signs of fracture till the day we die.

But the troubles we feel so personally are not ours alone. We are a community of the ailing, and the more we can discover and connect with its other fascinating, consoling members, the less our troubles will weigh on us as singular punishments. The mood of society as a whole may tend remorselessly towards cheeriness. We have access to a dark cheerfulness of our own, shared among fellow sufferers, who are equally resolute in meeting a fate they never asked for, do not deserve, but will refuse to be cowed by.

14.
Scepticism

Few things come more naturally to us than trust in our own minds: their first impressions, the feelings they summon up for us, their judgements about people and situations, their assessments of who we are, what we are worth and what the future may be like for us. It feels right and normal that we should accept, without hesitation or compunction, whatever response these minds put forward to consciousness. Why would we go to the trouble and tedium of starting to doubt what we innately and automatically think and feel? We must surely be able to trust our very own thinking machines.

Yet at the core of recovery from mental illness is the continually bewildering realisation that our minds are, at key moments, unreliable and illogical. To compound the problem, they give us no sign that they might be any such things. They insist on their reasonableness even while they are behaving in what we can only much later deduce, with great patience and effort, are foolish, harmful or demented ways. We have a grave enemy and deceiver right between our ears.

For example, these minds will tell us with total sincerity that the future holds something awful for us and will thereby ruin decades of our lives in paranoid obsessions and compulsive rituals. They will tell us with supreme confidence that we face grave danger by doing something that actually doesn't imperil us and might even bring us a chance to flourish. They will encourage us to sabotage relationships filled with love and possibility and drive willing partners from our arms. They will tell us to give up on promising work projects for fear we'll annoy someone, and will inform us that there is grave danger in building up faith in ourselves.

Our brains cannot think straight because they are reasoning via experiences in the past that were anomalous, unfair, unrepresentative and unreliable. These brains claim to know that we are useless because that is how we happened to be viewed by one or two caregivers when we were very small and our neural networks were being laid down. They have complete assurance that achieving success will be dangerous for us because it once was, for a little while, around a jealous and inadequate relative who died many years ago. These brains keep sabotaging our relationships because of one relationship that hurt us immensely when we were too young to know how to defend ourselves. Or they keep us in a subservient position with regard to someone in the present because this was once the safest way to be, when we were under five.

Our flawed brains are fateful generalisers from their earliest moments. They take the raw material of our young lives and extrapolate universal theories from them that can destroy our chances of responding adequately to the diverse and novel conditions of adult reality.

Recovering mental health depends on doing something counter-intuitive: doubting our first thoughts on pretty much all topics through an appreciation of our innate biases, how they are structured and where they came from. We should put a large distance between ourselves and any impulse that washes over us. Strong feelings – that we have found our ideal life partner after ten minutes, that we must leave a person immediately, that we are about to be destroyed, that everyone hates us, that disaster is upon us – should invariably be resisted, placed in a safe zone and inspected with the utmost rigour, calm and scepticism. We should develop an ingrained suspicion of our greatest, most spontaneous certainties, asking a whole series of questions of them: Is it really true that they told me they hate me? Did they actually say they wanted to end the relationship? Is there real evidence that everything is over?

It's a curious way to live and a humbling one too to have to pass our certainties through a constantly sceptical sieve and to demand that we sleep on conclusions and discuss them with a reliable friend before acting on them.

At given moments, especially when we are tired, we should realise that we are not capable of thinking correctly and should therefore stop thinking altogether rather than mangle our conclusions any further. We should hold on to the idea that when we are especially distressed and upset, we will have lost our hold on the fragile thread of reason.

There will be certain ideas that enter consciousness that, with politeness, we should just refuse to engage with, because we have done so too many times before and know they are futile and disconnected from anything real. There is no point in thinking, for the millionth time, about how ugly we are, how bad we are, how guilty we are. These aren't thoughts that have anything sensible to tell us about our lives today. With due respect to our minds, we'd be better off putting on some music, counting to a hundred or calling up a friend.

We'll be on the road to recovery and sanity when we see that one way to be properly reasonable is to appreciate how much of the time we aren't able to be so. We aren't disrespecting ourselves; we're properly honouring our complex histories and the congenitally flawed thinking patterns they have unwittingly led us to.

Conclusion: Living Long Term with Mental Illness

We would, of course, like any encounter with mental illness to be as brief as possible and, most importantly, to be isolated and singular. But the reality is that, for many of us, the illness will threaten to return for visits throughout our lives and it will be a condition to which we remain permanently susceptible. So, the challenge isn't to learn to survive only a one-off crisis; it's to set in place a framework that can help us to manage our fragility over the long term. Some of the following moves, practical and psychological, suggest themselves:

Acknowledgement

Being ready for a return of the illness will help us to calibrate our expectations and render us appropriately patient and unfrightened in the face of relapses. We should beware of the special price we have to pay when we have allowed ourselves to declare the battle over, when we have announced to ourselves and to friends that we are well again – and then recognise that we have actually been hasty and naïve and need to return to the front once more. It can feel especially bitter to have to crouch low again when we felt we now had the right to stand tall. Better to adopt a stance of ongoing, permanent readiness rather than submit to cycles of hope followed by panic. We fell ill over many years – our whole childhood might have been the incubating laboratory – and it should not surprise us if we are never totally impervious again.

Vigilance

We'll need to monitor ourselves with special care, vigilant for signs of deterioration and vortices of despair. Our minds are prone to amnesia; we forget what we have learnt about ourselves and what has kept us steady. We may have worked out the basic structure of our illness in therapy. We might know that we are prone to self-sabotage, that we carry a trauma with us from the past, that we are inclined to destroy everything that is good about our lives and alienate those who want to care for us. But such knowledge will always be vulnerable to destructive impulses that can sweep away our patient intellectual labour and catapult us back into a state of helpless and frightened infancy. We should be ready to be submerged by negativity, and not experience our retreat as a humiliation, confident that ebbs and flows are normal and that we will be able to hold on to at least some of our gains.

Repetition

Our minds don't just need good lessons, they need to learn good habits; that is, they need to fashion routines in which helpful rituals, activities and ideas are repeated until they become second nature. Like someone learning a new language, we need to go over certain points again and again, rehearsing notions of self-love, self-forgiveness, kindness and self-acceptance on a daily basis. Things are so slow because we aren't just trying to acquire intellectual concepts (something that might only need a minute); we're trying to alter our personalities. It will be a life's work.

Mental management

We need to be rigorous with our patterns of thinking. We cannot afford to let our thoughts wander into any old section of the mind. There are thoughts that we need to nurture – about our worth, about our right to be, about the importance of keeping going, about self-forgiveness. And there are thoughts we should be ruthless in chasing out – about how some people are doing so much better than us, about how inadequate and pitiful we are, about what a disappointment we have turned out to be. The latter aren't even 'thoughts'; they have no content to speak of, they cannot teach us anything new. They are really just instruments of torture and symptoms of a difficult past.

A support network

For the mentally fragile, a decent social life is not a luxury or a piece of entertainment. It is a resource to help us to stay alive. We need people to balance our minds when we are slipping. We need friends who will soothe our fears and not accuse us of self-indulgence or self-pity for the amount of time our illness has sequestered us. It will help immensely if they have struggles of their own and if we can therefore meet as equal fellow ailing humans, as opposed to hierarchically separated doctors and patients.

We'll need ruthlessness in expunging certain other people from our diaries: people who harbour secret resentments against us, who are latently hostile to self-examination, who are scared of their own minds and project their fears onto us. A few hours with such types can throw a shadow over a whole day; their unsympathetic voices become lodged in our minds and feed our own ample stores of self-doubt. We shouldn't hesitate to socially edit our lives in order to endure.

Vulnerability

When things are darkening, the impulse is to hide ourselves away and reduce communication. We are too ashamed to do anything else. We should fight the tendency and, precisely when we cannot bear to admit what we are going through, we should dare to take someone into our confidence. Silence is the primordial enemy. We have to fight a permanent feeling that we are too despicable to be looked after. We have to gamble on an always implausible idea: that we deserve kindness.

Love

Love is ultimately what will get us through – not romantic love, but sympathy, tolerance and patience. We'll need to watch our tendencies to turn love down from an innate sense of unworthiness. We wouldn't have become ill if it were easy for us to accept the positive attention of others. We'll have to thank those who are offering it and make them feel appreciated in return – and, most of all, accept that our illness was from the outset rooted in a deficit of love and therefore that every encounter with the emotion will strengthen our recovery and help to keep the darkness at bay.

Medication

We would prefer not to keep adding foreign chemicals to our minds. There are side effects and the eerie sense of not knowing exactly where our thoughts end and neurochemistry begins. But the ongoing medicines set up guard rails around the worst of our mental whirlpools. We may have to be protected on an ongoing basis from forces inside us that would prefer we didn't exist.

A quiet life

In our stronger moments, we may want to take on the world again and revive our largest ambitions. We should be careful of our motives. We don't need to be extraordinary to deserve to be. We should see the glory and the grandeur that is present in an apparently modest destiny. We are good enough as we are. We don't need huge sums of money or to be spoken of well by strangers. We need time to sort out our minds, and peace to stabilise our nerves. We must have hours free in which we can process our feelings and, lying in bed or in the bath, soothe our frightened minds. We should take pride in our early nights and undramatic routines. These aren't signs of passivity or tedium. What looks like a normal life on the outside is a singular achievement given what we are wrestling within.

Humour

There is no need for gravity. We can face down the illness by laughing heartily at its evils. We are 'mad' and 'cracked' and can say so honestly – but luckily so are many others with whom we can wryly mock the absurdities of mental life. We shouldn't, on top of everything else, accord our illness too much portentous respect.

Small and big wins

Many of the steps we take towards recovery could appear relatively small: a week in which we have not denigrated ourselves, a relationship in which we are allowing ourselves to enjoy kindness, a peaceful sequence of evenings ... The temptation might be to brush off these achievements too lightly for our own good. Given what we may have gone through, these are milestones that deserve celebration and commemoration so that we can notice how far we have come and gain strength from a glance back at the peaks and troughs of our mental lives.

In this context, we can think of the work of the English walking artist Hamish Fulton (born 1946), who has spent his long career making large black-and-white photographs of places in the world where he has walked. Some of these walks have been epic in scale (whole weeks spent trekking across the Himalayas and the Andes); others have been more domestic (a few hours in the Welsh mountains). But Fulton always accompanies his images with solemn text, a written record of where he has been, how many miles he went and how long it took him. He arrests a moment that might ordinarily be lost and lends it weight and dignity. Through immaculate lettering and sober photography, Fulton signals to us how much a walk may be life-changing, and as worthy of commemoration as a battle or a premiership.

One could imagine performing a similar exercise of commemoration on the business of recovering from mental illness. Here too there are plenty of moments that are quietly arduous and important, and that would warrant being frozen and highlighted. We could picture a vast photograph of an ordinary bathtub to which a caption might say: '12th May, evening, two hours of soaking, rethinking my relationship to what other people think.' Or a picture of an armchair by a window: '3rd September, an hour reflecting on my right to be

Hamish Fulton, *Walking to Benicadell, Spain*, 2016

Hamish Fulton, *A Five Day Circular Clockwise Walk Round London*, 2011

free and content.' A shot of an unmade bed at night might say: 'An evening of self-forgiveness.'

We should be proud of ourselves for making it this far. At times it may have looked as if we never would. There might have been nights when we sincerely thought of taking our own lives. Somehow we held on, we reached out for help, we dared to tell someone else of our problems, we engaged our minds, we tried to piece together our histories and to plot a more endurable future – and we started reading about what might be up with our minds. We are still here, mentally ill no doubt at times, but more committed than ever to recovery, appreciative of the light, grateful for love, hungry for insight and keen to help anyone else whose plight we can recognise. We are not fully well, but we are on the mend and that, for now, is good enough.

Picture credits

Cover
Vincent Van Gogh (1853-1889), *The Cypress and the Flowering Tree*, 1889. Private Collection

p. 17
Cy Twombly, *Synopsis of a Battle*, 1968. Oil and wax crayon on canvas, 172 cm × 207 cm. © Cy Twombly Foundation

p. 18
Artepics / Alamy Stock Photo

p. 19
Vincent van Gogh, *The Garden of Saint-Paul Hospital*, 1889. Oil on canvas, 95 cm × 75.5 cm. Kröller-Müller Museum, Otterlo, Netherlands / Wikimedia Commons

p. 29t
Francisco Goya, *Yard with Lunatics*, 1794. Oil on tin-plated iron, 43.8 cm × 32.7 cm. The Meadows Museum, Dallas, USA / Wikimedia Commons

p. 29b
Everett Collection Historical / Alamy Stock Photo

p. 31
Tea bowl, Ichinyu-Raku IV (possibly), c. 1600–1699. Black glaze, 8.4 cm × 12 cm. Rijksmuseum, Amsterdam, Netherlands

p. 32
Tea bowl, White Satsuma ware, Edo period, 17th century. Stoneware with clear, crackled glaze, stained by ink; gold lacquer repairs, 10.5 cm × 12.2 cm. Freer Gallery of Art, Washington, DC., USA. Gift of Charles Lang Freer

p. 35
Gwen John, *Self Portrait*, 1902. Oil on canvas, 34.9 cm × 44.8 cm. Tate Gallery, London, England / Wiki Art

p. 60
Joseph Mallord William Turner, *Valley of Aosta: Snowstorm, Avalanche, and Thunderstorm*, c. 1836–1837. Oil on canvas, 92.2 cm × 123 cm. Art Institute of Chicago, Chicago, USA. Frederick T. Haskell Collection / Wikimedia Commons

p. 62
Vilhelm Hammershøi, *Interior in Strandgade, Sunlight on the Floor*, 1901. Oil on canvas, 46.5 cm × 52 cm. SMK, Copenhagen, Denmark / Wikimedia Commons

p. 64
John Pawson, The Life House, Wales, 2016. Photograph by Gilbert McCarragher. Image courtesy of Living Architecture

p. 91
Ferdinand Hodler, *The Disappointed Souls*, 1892. Oil on canvas, 120 cm × 299 cm. Guggenheim Museum, New York, USA. Album / Alamy Stock Photo

p. 91
Ferdinand Hodler, *The Disappointed Souls*, 1892. Oil on canvas, 120 cm × 299 cm. Guggenheim Museum, New York, USA. Album / Alamy Stock Photo

p. 107
© Chino Otsuka, *1980 and 2009, Nagayama, Japan,* from the series *Imagine Finding Me*, 2009

p. 108
© Chino Otsuka, *1982 and 2005, Paris, France,* from the series *Imagine Finding Me*, 2005

p. 109
© Chino Otsuka, *1976 and 2005, Kamakura, Japan,* from the series *Imagine Finding Me*, 2005

p. 133
Gustave Caillebotte, *The Yerres, Effect of Rain*, 1875. Oil on canvas, 80.3 cm × 59.1 cm. Sidney and Lois Eskenazi Museum of Art, Indiana University, USA / Wikimedia Commons

p. 136
Anonymous, *The Yongzheng Emperor Admiring Flowers*, c. 1725. Palace Museum, Beijing, China / Public domain

p. 142
Katsushika Hokusai, *Mishima Pass in Kai Province (Kōshū Mishima goe)*, from the series *Thirty-six Views of Mount Fuji,* c. 1830–1832. Woodblock print; ink and colour on paper, 24.8 cm × 37.5 cm. Metropolitan Museum of Art, New York, USA / Wikimedia Commons

p. 144
Pierre Belon, a page from *Histoire de la Nature des Estranges Poissons Marins*, 1551 / Wikimedia Commons

p. 170
Hamish Fulton, *Walking To Benicadell, Spain*, 2016. Walking On The Iberian Peninsular. Bombas Gens catalogue page 2018. Image courtesy of Hamish Fulton

p. 171
Hamish Fulton, *A Five Day Circular Clockwise Walk Round London*, 2011. Ink jet limited edition print. Image courtesy of Hamish Fulton

We hope you have found the content of this book helpful. This book is not intended to be a substitute for professional advice, diagnosis or treatment and is not appropriate for emergencies. Always seek the advice of a qualified health provider with any questions you may have regarding your mental health. If you think you may have a medical or mental health emergency, call 999 (UK) or 911 (US) immediately, or go to the nearest open clinic or emergency room.

The School of Life offers online therapy as a resource to help people feel supported. Our psychotherapists and psychologists are all fully accredited practitioners, registered with tightly governed professional UK bodies. For more information on our therapy services, please visit:

www.theschooloflife.com/therapy

The School of Life is a global organisation helping people lead more fulfilled lives. It is a resource for helping us understand ourselves, for improving our relationships, our careers and our social lives – as well as for helping us find calm and get more out of our leisure hours. We do this through films, workshops, books, apps, gifts and community. You can find us online, in stores and in welcoming spaces around the globe.

THESCHOOLOFLIFE.COM